Walking
The Western Isles

Clan Walk Guides

Walking
The Western Isles

Mary Welsh
maps and illustrations by
Christine Isherwood

First published Westmorland Gazette, 1993 as
Walks in the Western Isles
Revised edition published by Clan Books, 1999
Reprinted 2003
This new re-titled edition published by Clan Books, 2006

ISBN 1 873597 27 4
Text © Mary Welsh 2006
Maps and Illustrations © Christine Isherwood 2006

Clan Books
Clandon House
The Cross, Doune
Perthshire
FK16 6BE

Printed and bound in Great Britain by
St. Edmundsbury Press, Bury St. Edmunds, Suffolk

Introduction

The Western Isles—more romantically known as the Outer Hebrides—lie 120 miles / 190km off the north-western coast of Scotland and stretch for 130 miles / 210km from the Butt of Lewis to Barra Head. Here the walker in search of tranquillity and solitude can wander all day over dramatic hills and awesome moorland enjoying the magnificent seascapes without meeting another person. There are hundreds of islands in the archipelago, varying greatly in size.

Lewis

Lewis and Harris form a single island, largest of the Western Isles. Lewis is made up of rolling moors pitted with freshwater lochs and gouged by long sea lochs. It has low hills to the south west, glorious sands and cliffs along its indented west coast and great seascapes on its east coast, with views to the Sutherland Hills.

Harris

Common Sandpiper

Harris has its own unique physical characteristics. It is a land of high mountains with barely a cupful of soil. It has spectacular waterfalls, hidden lochs and miles of magnificent sands, behind which stretch the machair, unbelievably beautiful, with a myriad of summer flowers. The island of Scalpay is linked to North Harris by a bridge.

North Uist

The countryside of North Uist consists of heather moorland surrounding innumerable lochs. These are brilliantly revealed from the tops of the hills that form its rocky spine. The east coast is riven with sea lochs and from this coast there are wonderful views of the Isle of Skye. To the west lie great beaches of shell-sand. The lovely island of Berneray is linked to North Uist by a causeway.

Benbecula

A flat land of heathery peat moors, Benbecula's coasts are indented and there are many sandy beaches. From the top of its hills it looks as if with one big tide the island might float out to sea. It is sandwiched between the two Uists and linked to them by causeways.

Wheatear

South Uist

South Uist is the second largest island of the Western Isles. Its west coast is one long sandy beach, rarely breached. Behind the sand stretches the wide machair, ideal for farming and crofting. Between the machair and the island's mountainous spine lies a peaty moorland pocked with freshwater lochs. Its east coast is pierced by three large sea lochs, Boisdale, Eynort and Skipport. These are overlooked by South Uist's two handsome high peaks, Ben Mhor and Hecla. Their steepish slopes extend down to the rocky cliffs of the east coast. The island of Eriskay is linked to South Uist by a causeway. The ferry for Barra leaves Eriskay's west coast, from a terminal close to Prince Charlie's Bay.

Barra

The island's main centre is Castlebay. The houses, shops, community school, churches, hotels and library nestle on the edge of a huge natural harbour. A short distance off shore, on a small island, stands Kisimul Castle, ancient seat of the Clan MacNeil. Today the castle is leased to Historic Scotland. The magnificent sands of the Eoligarry peninsula are famous for their cockles, and the island's airport is there.

Acknowledgement

My thanks go to VisitScotland, WalkingWild and Caledonian MacBrayne, which gave me considerable support when I was re-walking and revising this book and seeking out new walks to enhance the contents. My grateful thanks also go to Dr Catherine Isherwood and Patrick Isherwood, who tirelessly checked routes from Butt to Vatersay. Christine Isherwood, their mother, who illustrates my walking books with such a sure and sympathetic touch, has once again greatly enhanced the text of this one with her delightful illustrations and accurate, detailed maps. Lastly my thanks must go to my husband Tom, who encourages me on every mile (from his armchair) and is such a support.

The Gaelic Today

All the directions on the signposts in the Western Isles are given only in Gaelic. The Ordnance Survey Explorer maps also use only Gaelic. In this book, for the first reference to the names of towns, villages, tiny settlements and hills I have given the English names first and then the Gaelic, in brackets. Thereafter I have used the Anglicised name, and only rarely the Gaelic for a second time. When giving the Gaelic names, I have used the spellings shown on the Explorer maps. These may differ from the spellings used on the signposts, which, in turn may differ from those used by local people. There is a move afoot to standardise the spellings but this is not proving to be very popular.

Lapwings

Whalebone Arch at Bragar
(see page 23)

Author's Note

Please remember on all these walks:

Wear suitable clothes and take adequate waterproofs.

Walk in strong footwear; walking boots are advisable.

Carry the relevant map and know how to use it.

Take extra food and drink as emergency rations.

Carry a whistle; remember six long blasts repeated at one minute intervals is the distress signal.

Do not walk alone, and tell someone where you are going.

If mist descends, return.

Keep all dogs under strict control. Observe all 'No Dogs' notices - they are there for very good reasons.

Terns

Readers are advised that while the author has taken every effort to ensure the accuracy of this guidebook, changes can occur after publication. You should check locally on transport, accommodation, etc. The publisher would welcome notes of any changes. Neither the publisher nor the author can accept responsibility for errors, omissions or any loss or injury.

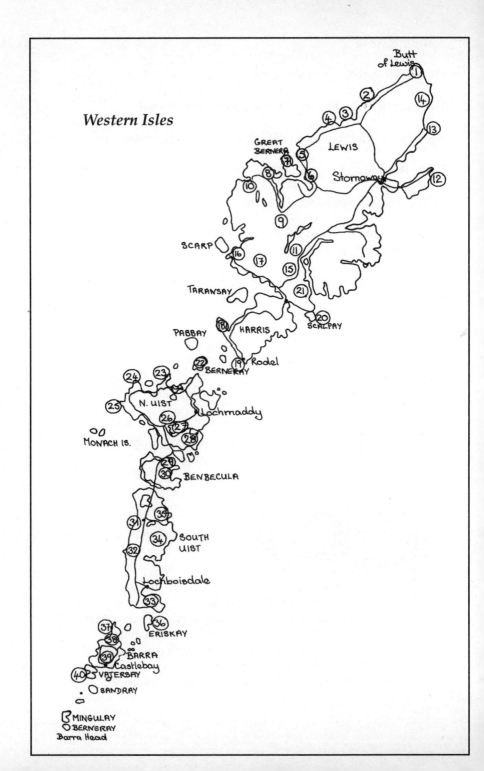

Western Isles

Contents

Contents continued page 10

1

Butt of Lewis (Rubha Robhanais), Isle of Lewis (Eilean Leodhais)

Park close to the church or the old school at Lionel (Lional), on the B8013, grid ref. 523642. This is reached by taking the A857 to Lionel and then turning left onto the B-road. Lionel lies 28 miles north of Stornoway (Steornabhagh).

At the most northerly point of Lewis, 'the sharp-end' of the island, stands the **Butt of Lewis lighthouse** regularly featured in weather reports from coastal stations. It overlooks awesome cliffs and often stormy seas. The lighthouse was built by Thomas Stevenson in 1862. Below the towering light stand the support buildings, painted a brilliant white, with yellow surrounds to windows and doors. It was automated in 1998.

Butt of Lewis

St Molua's Church (Teampall Mholuaidh) is approached by a gated way over croftland, about 200m north of Eoropie (Eoropaidh) village. It is believed to have been built in the twelfth century. It is dedicated to St Molua who may have first preached Christianity in Lewis in the sixth century. Photographs taken of the church before it was restored in 1912 show it as roofless but with its four main walls almost intact.

Machair is a Gaelic word for coastal grassland of the north and west of Scotland. It is formed by wind blowing shell sand inland over thousands of years. Masses of flowers and grasses mix with corn grown as winter feed for cattle and sheep. Machair supports large numbers of nesting wading birds.

Walk 1

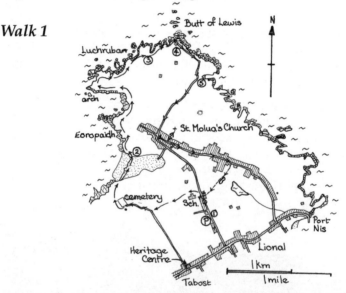

1 From the old school, walk down the road and turn left just beyond the police station. Continue past the school, along a fenced grassy sward, which in summer is colourful with flowers. On joining a tarmac road, turn right, to walk along it as it crosses the machair. This leads to the cemetery, placed like so many on Lewis, on a slope close to the sea. Stroll beside the cemetery and on to pass the radio mast. Turn right (north) and walk around the lovely sandy bay of Eoropie, where the great dark-blue Atlantic rollers turn to white foaming surf. Look for the natural arch in the jutting headland, known as the Eye of the Butt.

2 Pass through the gate on the far side of the bay and bear left to begin the pleasing walk around the indented coastline. Look left to see the tidal rocky island of Luchruban. Legend tells that in prehistoric times it was inhabited by pygmies or small folk. Continue along the low cliffs, where the waves crash onto the rocky shoreline, and climb a stile over the next fence. Oystercatchers sit on rocks, facing in the same direction, and piping loudly. Sea thrift colours the sward. Ahead, the cliffs become high and sheer and the folded Lewisian Gneiss rock (which forms most of Lewis) is well displayed. Here you should proceed with care.

3 Stride on over the springy turf and along the cliffs to climb a stile that gives access to the pasture around the Butt. Walk on to see the lighthouse. Sit on a rock and enjoy this dramatic point, where great expanses of ocean stretch away to the north, east and west. Watch the numerous seabirds nesting on the awesome cliffs. All their noise and movement is a delight to hear and see.

4 Leave the Butt by the narrow road. Look left to see more interesting folding of the pink Lewisian Gneiss, Scotland's most ancient rock. Follow the road as it curves inland and passes through an extensive area of lazy-beds. These were formed, in times gone by, by crofters who dug long straight ditches and piled soil and seaweed upon the land between, providing extra soil for their crops, mainly potatoes, and improving drainage.

Thrift

5 Continue past a delightful sandy bay and walk on. On reaching the crossroads, turn left to pass between the modern houses and bungalows of Eoropie. Outside each stands a large stack of peat, each cut in the typical Lewis shape. Look for the sign for St Molua's Church. Episcopalian services are occasionally held in this lovely simple building. Go inside and enjoy its peace. Walk on along the road until you approach the signpost for the township of Knockaird (An Cnoc Ard). Here turn right and pass between the houses to a stile to the machair.

Head on towards the road opposite and pass through a gate to the left of the church hall. Turn left up the road to where you have parked.

6 You may wish to turn left and walk on to visit the interesting Ness Heritage Centre at Habost (Tabost). This adds 1 ¼ miles in each direction to the walk as the heritage centre is at the place marked 'Mus' on the map. You might prefer to drive there after the walk rather than walk there!

Oystercatchers

Practicals

Type of walk: A delightful walk. Great sea views, dramatic cliffs, a lighthouse and a restored ancient chapel—a good walk. Generally easy walking all the way. Children under control on the cliffs.

Distance: 6 ½ miles / 10.5km
Time: 3–4 hours
Maps: OS Explorer 460 / Landranger 8

2

Shader (Siadar), Lewis

Park at the shore end of road at Shader, grid ref. 380549. To access this turn left (west), off the A857

Clach an Truiseil, the largest monolith in the north of Scotland, 20 ft / 6m high stands in the village of Ballantrushal (Baile an Truiseil), 13 miles north west of Stornoway. As you look at it, ponder on how it could have been levered into position by ancient folk without the help of modern equipment. It is believed that it might have been a guide in prehistoric times for boats wishing to land at the nearby beach. Tradition says that the stone marks the site of those killed in a battle between the Morrisons of Ness (Nis) and MacAulays of Uig but it is, of course, of a much earlier date than the clans.

The dun on a small island in **Loch an Duin** gives it its name. It is reached by a sketchy causeway. When in use, possibly 2,000 years ago, it would have had a series of 'dropping stones' along its length. If these were stepped on, the rock would have made a noise to warn the inhabitants of strangers approaching. Those who knew their location would have avoided these noisy stones. Nearby on a low hill

Clach an Truiseil

15

overlooking the loch is the Neolithic chambered cairn, Steinacleit, which dates from around 3000 to 5000 BC. To the north-east stands Clach Stei Lin, another lichen-clad standing stone. These two sites together with the two standing stones suggest that this area was well populated in prehistoric times. Near to where you have parked are the remains of the ruined early Christian church, Teampall Pheadair.

1 Return along the road, in summer past stands of yellow iris and

Walk 2

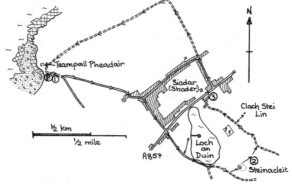

monkey flower, through the small crofting township of Shader to the A857 and cross to continue ahead along a lane. Where the fence turns away left, follow it to come close to Loch an Duin to view the causeway leading out to the dun. Return to the lane and turn left. Go through a signposted gate and continue up the good track onto the little hillock to see the remains of the chambered cairn, Steinacleit, from where there is a fine view of the loch and its dun.

2 Stroll a small footpath, north-east, away from the hillock across the pasture, well to the right of a small conifer plantation, to reach a fence which you climb. Walk left beside it to go through a gate to join a track and turn left. Follow the track as it bends right and then go on ahead to pass behind the plantation. At the end of the trees, take a gate on your right and cross the field to visit Clach Stei Lin. Return to the track and walk right to follow it back to the A-road.

3 Cross and turn right and then left to take a lane, passing left of the school. Where the lane turns sharp left, go on ahead along a track. This takes you gently uphill before turning sharply left to lead between crofts, with ruined blackhouses particularly on the seaward

16

side. Look out for golden plovers, lapwings and ruff as you pass the fields, and the impressive spikes of the northern marsh orchis. As you near the sea, look to your right to see the ruined foundations of Teampall Pheadair, which can be reached by a short walk across the pasture. Return to the track and continue to your car. Then drive back to the A-road, turn right and take the right turn for Ballantrushal to see the magnificent standing stone.

Northern
Marsh Orchid

Practicals

Type of walk: Lots to see. Some road, lane, track and pasture walking required to see these ancient sites

Distance: 3 ½ miles / 5.5km
Time: 2 hours
Maps: OS Explorer 460 / Landranger 8

3

Barvas (Barabhas) and Brue (Bru) Walkways, Lewis

Park at the end of Loch Street (Sraid an Loch), Barvas, grid ref. 348505. To access this leave Stornoway by the A857, towards Ness. At Barvas, continue round a sharp right-hand bend to take Loch Street, the first turning on the left.

Apparently in 1585, **3,000 salmon** were taken out of the Barvas river. It was considered the best salmon river in Lewis and special precautions were taken to preserve its fertility.

Rinn Mollerap - cliffs and sea stacks

1 From the parking area, follow a sandy vehicle track towards the sea until you can cross a concrete bridge. Turn immediately left and follow either track along the machair until you reach an abandoned green bus (!); pass this and proceed down to the river, the outlet for large Loch Mor Barvas (Loch Mor Bharabhais), which can be crossed by a footbridge. Follow the way-marked posts to your right, away from the track, to pass on your right a small stone circle around a pool with a burial cairn in the centre. Rejoin the track. Then take a footpath along the side of the fence with the way-marked posts to your right until you reach a paved road with a parking area and a view over Loch Ereray (Eirearaigh). Notices request that you do not disturb ground nesting birds on the spit, which separates the loch from the sea.

Walk 3

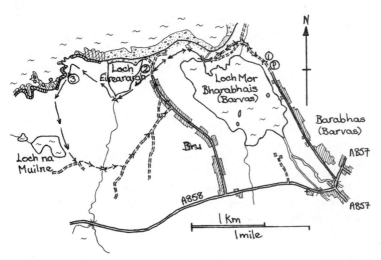

2 Follow the way-marked footpath beside the fence as it leads you towards the loch. Pass through two gates then cross a sturdy footbridge over the River Ereray (Abhainn Eirearaigh) where it enters the loch. Continue along the loch shore round towards the sea before striking diagonally up the hill across old peat workings towards the next way-mark, staying outside the fenced enclosures.

19

Follow the way-marks round the fence corner towards the cliffs before turning left again to continue up the hill. For the intrepid, it is possible to walk rather closer to the cliff edge to get a lovely view over the skerries and sea stacks in the bays, keeping the way-posts in sight to your left—but be careful as the edge of the cliffs are crumbly. The cliffs play host to many nesting seabirds, especially fulmars.

Greenshank

3 Follow the coast round over Rinn Mollerap and down into a shallow valley. Head gradually inland to make for the stile over the fence by a fence junction, and follow the way-marks along beside the fence across old peat cuttings. To your right you will see Loch na Muilne, with stands of bog bean, and the distant houses of Arnol. The way posts lead you past the loch to a peat track, which you cross, and on over more old peat cuttings with faint traces of the path. Cross a wooden footbridge over the River Ereray and continue slanting left to meet a distinct footpath coming in from your left. This leads you on to a good vehicle track on which you turn left.

4 Follow the track towards Brue village. At the edge of the village, take the right fork and continue to the road. Turn left and make your way down to the road end beside Loch Ereray, where you rejoin your outward route and retrace your steps back round Loch Mor Barvas.

Practicals

Type of walk: This is a pleasing walk, with lots of fine views. It can be muddy in parts after rain.

Distance: 5 ½ miles / 9km
Time: 3–4 hours
Maps: OS Explorer 460 / Landranger 8

4

Arnol, Lewis

Park at the end of the road beyond the Blackhouse Museum, Arnol, grid ref. 311496. Take care not to block any vehicles using this area as a turning point. The village is situated just off the A858 on the west coast of Lewis.

The name **blackhouse** has been in use since the 1840s. It is used to describe any house in the Western Isles that was constructed with double drystone walls and a thatched roof. The gap between the double walls was filled with earth. The roof, resting on the inner wall, was covered with straw thatch although in some areas heather or turfs were used. This thatch was held in place by heather ropes and weighted down with anchor stones.

The **last blackhouses** were built early in the twentieth century and some were lived in as late as the 1980s. The house had a single entrance for the family and their beasts. Once inside a line of stones divided the two but later an internal wall replaced the stones. Originally beds were let into the wall around the central hearth. But from the 1850s wooden box beds came into fashion replacing the wall beds. These were curtained to give some degree of privacy.

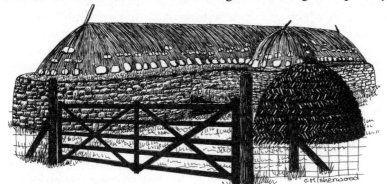

Blackhouse, Arnol

1 From the parking area at the end of the road, beyond Arnol and the blackhouse, walk on along the cart track, keeping to the right of a dwelling. Continue towards the shore. Pass through a gate in the fence on the left, beyond which, in the summer, grows a large clump of field gentians. Go through a gap in the low sod wall and make for the cliffs overlooking a rocky bay where Atlantic rollers crash white-topped on the jagged rocks. Head left along the lovely cliffs, with the sea to your right, walking over a carpet of pink thrift in summer. Go on past little Arnol Island. Follow the path that keeps to the right of the fence and runs to the left of a huge spit of boulders stretching across Arnol Bay. In summertime, in the lea of this large natural breakwater, grows a myriad of flowers, including great patches of marsh cinquefoil and sea campion. The spit shelters Loch Arnol, with sandbanks emerging above its placid waters. Out on the rocky shore you might see men collecting winkles and taking them away in their tractors. Continue behind the spit until you come to the place where it is breached by the River Arnol flowing out of the loch.

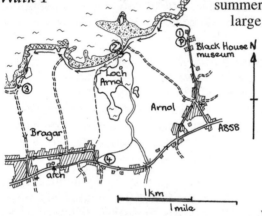

Walk 4

2 Step across on boulders—unless you are walking after several days of rain, in which case you will have to discard your boots and wade. If the river is in spate, you may be unable to cross and will have to return by your outward route. Or you might be able to use a suspension bridge, the construction of which is being discussed at the time of writing, as a way of helping walkers across the outflow. Carry on along the grassy track behind the vast wall of boulders. Cross the narrow road that leads from the shore to Bragar and stroll on along the grassy cliffs. Press on to Bragar Bay and move round the end of a fence where it ends on a rock. Follow a narrow path beyond that heads inland with the waters of the bay to your right. This path leads you to the lonely, walled cemetery of

Bragar.

3 Join the narrow, flower-lined road that runs inland to Bragar. At the T-junction, turn left and walk through the scattered township. As you near the A-road look for the huge jawbone of a blue whale that came ashore in 1920. The harpoon that killed it was still attached to its body. The arch was restored in 2001. Walk on to join the A858.

4 Turn left to continue along the generally quiet road for nearly a mile, to take the signposted left turn for the blackhouse. Hopefully you have allowed yourself time to visit the interpretative centre and the blackhouse. In the latter enjoy the open peat fire on the floor, its glorious smell pervading the house. When it was lived in the smoke would have escaped through the thatch, helping to preserve it from rotting in the damp. Many of the other recently occupied blackhouses had chimneys put in which led to problems with the thatching and this probably contributed to their decline. From the blackhouse walk on to where you have parked.

Sea Campion

Practicals

Type of walk: The blackhouse is extremely interesting. Easy walking for most of the way. Crossing the River Arnol might present problems. The walk along the A-road cannot be avoided as the ground to your left is too boggy to cross.

Distance: 5 miles / 8km
Time: 3–4 hours
Maps: OS Explorer 460 / Landranger 8

5

Carloway Broch
(Dun Charlabhaigh), Lewis

Park in the in the car park, where there are toilets, grid ref. 192412. To access this, drive west on the A858 and continue through Breasclete (Brescleit), where the coast is reached. After passing Loch an Dunain and the hotel beyond it, take the next left turn and drive along the road for a quarter of a mile.

Carloway Broch (Dun Charlabhaigh) dominates the surrounding crofting township of the same name on the west side of the Isle of Lewis. A broch is a circular defensive tower of the early Iron Age in Scotland, and Carloway broch is the best preserved example in the Western Isles.

Cross the road from the car park and climb the reinforced path towards the **interpretation centre**. Pass through a kissing gate and then wander at will. As you explore the broch notice the double walls that gave strength and stability to the construction. Pass through the low entrance and look for the cells between the walls, and for the staircase. A ledge running head-height round the inner wall would have supported a wooden gallery. Enjoy

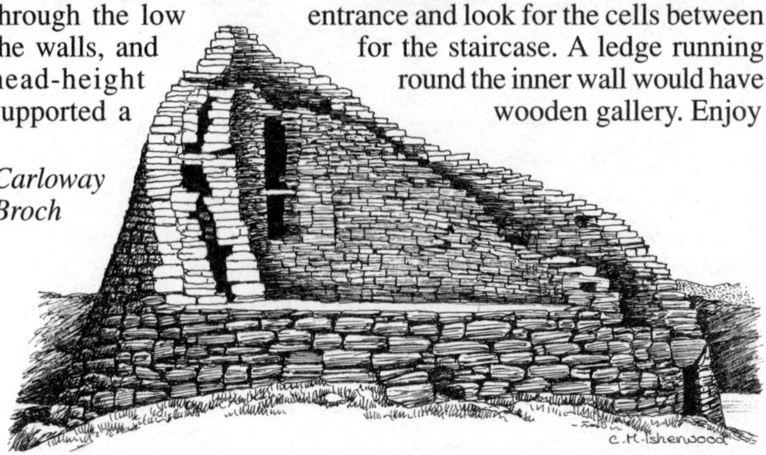

Carloway Broch

C.H. Isherwood

Walk 5

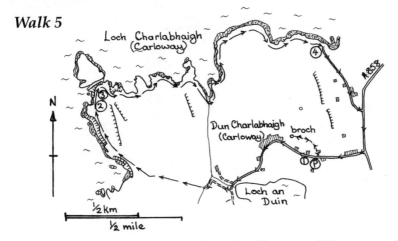

Loch Charlabhaigh (Carloway)

Dun Charlabhaigh (Carloway) broch

Loch an Duin

N

½ km

½ mile

A858

the stunning view from the broch, with glimpses of blue sea and loch.

1 After your explorations return to the road, and walk on, right, to its end by Loch an Duin, noticing the blackhouses as you and the ruins to be seen along both sides. Once over the culvert at the end, turn right to walk a wide track towards a derelict crofthouse. Follow the track as it swings left, keeping the fence to the right. At the end of the fence, cross a small stream by a stone footbridge. Then, bearing steadily right (north), with the sea to your left, begin your climb up the slope of Creag Mhor. At the top is a breath-taking view of East Loch Roag (Loch Rog an Ear) and of Great and Little Bernera, with their accompanying rocks and tiny islands.

2 Descend to the greensward on the cliffs below. Turn right, north, and begin a gentle stroll along the cliffs, looking ahead for the easiest and, occasionally, the safest way, with the sea still to the left. Here you might see bog pimpernel thriving in the damp areas and find field gentians on the drier slopes. Look out to sea for gannets diving. Continue along the cliffs until you reach a headland at the entrance to Loch Carloway (Loch Charlabhaigh). Here is the place to sit to enjoy this lovely stretch of coast.

3 Head on round the cliff tops, with Loch Carloway now to your left, using animal tracks, which help you to find the easiest way. On reaching a fence, keep to the loch side of it. Soon a narrow path continues outside the fence as it comes close to a large bay. Where a small landslip has occurred, climb the stile and then climb back

25

over another to regain the path beyond the slip. Stroll on along the glorious low cliffs, where buzzards take off to soar overhead, keening as they go. Look left across the waters of the loch to see the curious stone walls of a field system of a century ago. Carry on until the Carloway pier comes into view. The narrow sheep-track descends to the water's edge, where a gate gives access to a narrow road.

Buzzard

4 Walk uphill, where in summer the way is bordered with flags, wild mint and ferns. Opposite a blackhouse, go through a gate on the right. Climb the low hill ahead to join an old grassy track below cliffs, where you walk left. Follow this until you reach a road. Go on ahead and then turn right at the end to return to the car park.

Practicals

Type of walk: The broch is a must for all visitors to Lewis. The walk around the coast is very pleasant. Generally easy walking, but some parts marshy after rain. Some steepish hill climbing. No real footpaths or way-marking but useful sheep trods.

Distance:	5 miles / 8km
Time:	2–3 hours. Allow extra time for exploring the broch
Maps:	OS Explorer 460 / Landranger 8

NB No dogs allowed

6

Callanish (Calanais) Stones and Two Stone Circles, Lewis

Park at the well signposted Callanish Stones Visitor Centre car park, 750m west, off the A858, grid ref. 214327, and 18 miles / 31.5km from Stornoway.

It is now believed that sometime between 3000 and 2000 BC a circular ditch was dug to enclose the area where the **Callanish (Calanais) stones** now stand. Later, in this enclosure cultivation ridges were dug for growing crops. On top of these ridges the ring of standing stones, the central monolith and the southern row were put in place. Some time later the chambered tomb, used for communal burial for several centuries, was built and later still the ceremonial avenue of stones and the remaining arms were added.

In 1857–8 **Sir James Matheson**, a former proprietor of Lewis, had much of the peat removed from around the stones. It had grown to a height of 6ft 5 inches, obscuring many. Since then more of the original form

Callanish stones

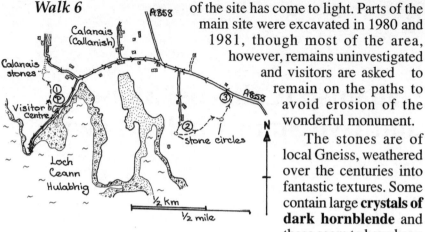

Walk 6

of the site has come to light. Parts of the main site were excavated in 1980 and 1981, though most of the area, however, remains uninvestigated and visitors are asked to remain on the paths to avoid erosion of the wonderful monument.

The stones are of local Gneiss, weathered over the centuries into fantastic textures. Some contain large **crystals of dark hornblende** and these seem to have been specially selected and probably held some significance for the people of that time.

1 From the visitor centre car park, follow the well made footpath leading up to the Callanish stones sited on the hilltop, where you will want to wander and enjoy this wonderful, magical corner of Lewis. Leave the site by the gate on the hilltop giving access to a narrow lane that leads steeply downhill. At the foot, turn left and follow the road back to the A858. Turn right and, after about 100m, right again along a small lane, which leads past a few houses to a small car park. Go through a gate and follow the narrow path across the field, looking out for old lazybeds, then take either the stile or gate to gain access to the stone circle Cnoc Ceann a' Gharraidh. This oval *Round-leaved* ring consists of five standing *& Long-leaved* stones, the tallest 12 ft high. *Sundew* When the site was cleared of peat in the late nineteenth century a cairn, sockets left by wooden posts and another stone, were revealed. From the circle look north-west to see the Callanish Stones on their hill, dominating the landscape.

28

2 Then look east to see another stone circle on raised ground. Follow the narrow path that leads across the wet pasture, crossing bridges over the worst of the marshy areas, to a stile over a fence. Beyond, follow the path up the hill to a larger circle of stones, Cnoc Fhillibhir Bheag. This circle consists of 12 stones, some 10 ft tall, of which four form an inner ring. Continue on the path towards the main road and notice the interesting gate giving access on to it.

3 Turn left and walk along the side of the A-road and then turn left towards the visitor centre. Ignore the turn into the car park and continue along the narrow road to the jetty at the end. From here there is a lovely view up Loch Ceann Hulabhig and across the loch to the two stone circles you have just visited. Then return along the road to the visitor centre and its excellent gift shop and cafe.

Red-throated Divers

Practicals

Type of walk: Your first view of the main circle is breathtaking. This delightful walk takes you on to two satellite circles, where the route can be a bit boggy but all easy walking

Distance: 2 ½ miles / 4km
Time: 2 hours
Maps: OS Explorer 459 / Landranger 8 and 13

7

Great Bernera (Bearnaraigh), Lewis

Park at the Bernera Community Centre, refreshments and toilets in season, grid ref. 158367. The island, 25 miles from Stornoway, is accessed by taking the A858 to Garynahine (Gearraidh na h-Aibhne) and then on along the B8011. Then take the B8059, which leads off on the right, signposted Earshader (Iarsiadar). Continue until you can cross the bridge (known as the bridge 'across the Atlantic') on to Great Bernera. Drive on ahead to the township of Breaclete (Breacleit), and the Community Centre.

Tob Bhalasaigh is a sheltered lagoon with a rare mixture of seaweeds found only in this unusual mix of salt and freshwater. The unusual footbridge was built in 1898 to provide access for the people who lived on the other side of the Tob. It is still difficult to transport goods across the bridge and this has resulted in people building new homes on the other side of the bridge.

In 1992 a severe storm exposed, from the machair behind Bosta (Bostadh) beach, a late **Iron Age village**. When the site was

Reconstructed Iron Age House, Great Bernera

Walk 7

excavated a series of semi-subterranean linked double walled drystone houses were revealed. They had no windows or doors. Each house had a long low entrance passage that led to a large circular room, with an open hearth. It is believed that the village was inhabited by Picts, dating from 1500 years ago or more. Later a Viking house was built over the ruins. This was a good position for a settlement as it was sheltered from the weather, and had fresh water, grazing and arable land. The people would have kept sheep, pigs, cattle for food and foraged for shellfish including limpets, oysters, mussels, scallops as well as fish.

A **life size reconstruction** of one of these houses can be seen nearby. It has been built using techniques that would have been available in the Iron Age. The entrance passage is curved to break high winds, with a slope down from the ground level to the house floor. The house is open to visitors on Mon–Fri between 12 noon and 4 p.m.

1 From the Community Centre walk for three-quarters of a mile, west, along the road to Hacklete (Tacleit) to take the right turn for Valasay (Bhalasaigh). Carry on to the end of the road, where you cross the unusual footbridge over the Tob Bhalasaigh. Look for the ruined houses deserted when people moved to the other side. Go past the first cottage and turn right. Follow the path leading you on through the next three gates. From now on follow the winding way-marked path along the lovely coast, with care, as it

31

curves round geos, inlets and gullies. Then continue on with Loch Veiravat to your right. Head on along the path until it winds right on an old track to join a narrow road at Tobson, the oldest inhabited settlement on Bernera. Turn left for a few steps and then left again, still on the road.

2 Pause in Tobson to look at several ruined crofthouses. Then follow the way-marked route up Beinn an Toib, going off right. Pause to get your breath back at the top and enjoy the spectacular view over Loch Roag. Carry on keeping to the left of several small lochs until you reach a gate. Go through and wind right to cross the outlet of the much larger loch to the right of the smaller ones just passed. Carry on down the glorious valley with the outflow stream to your left to pass the many ruins of the deserted village of Bosta. Here in summer the greensward is spangled with buttercups, marsh marigolds and ragged robin. Dawdle on come to the fine Bosta beach.

3 Here you will want to linger on the lovely sands and view the remains of the Iron-Age village and the reconstructed Iron-Age house. The wall tops of three houses remain uncovered, giving a clear indication of their layout. The site could not be left excavated due to the shifting nature of the sands and so had to be backfilled to protect it. There are toilets here, which are open all year. Then join the narrow road to walk east. Follow it as it winds on, with the sea to your left, and where it winds round right. Go past delectable Loch na Muilne. At the turning to Tobson, which you ignore, look for the memorial cairn to the crofters, who in April 1874, marched to the door of Lews Castle in Stornoway. Here they complained to Sir James Matheson about receiving eviction notices. Three men were sent for trial but were found not guilty and the eviction notices were withdrawn. Then continue on to the community centre.

Practicals

Type of walk: A lovely walk that seasoned walkers will enjoy. Keep to the way-marked paths and take care along the coastline. The rocky outcrops give your boots good purchase. Pleasing narrow, quiet road walking.

Distance:	7 ½ miles / 12km
Time:	4–5 hours
Maps:	OS Explorer 458 / 13

8

Kneep (Cnip) and Berie (Beirigh) Sands, Lewis

Park down the narrow road, opposite the phone box, to the small pier at Kneep, grid ref. 100358. To access this leave Stornoway as for walk 7. Continue on the B8011 along the west side of Little Loch Roag and then Loch Roag. Just before the start of Glen Valtos (Gleann Bhaltois), turn right and head north beside Loch Sgailer (Sgailleir). Pass through the settlement of Cliff (Cliobh) and then onto Kneep (Cnip) to choose a parking place that does not impede other vehicles.

The **gentian family** are all beautiful flowers. Field gentians are found on dunes, cliffs and meadows, where the soil is acid. The largish flowers are a bluish purple though sometimes white. They flower from July to September. Look for them in northern England, Scotland and Ireland, but in southern England they are very rare. During the summer, field gentians are seen early on this walk on the cliffs.

Berie Sands and West Cliffs

33

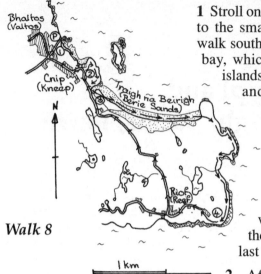

Bhaltos
(Valtos)

Cnip
(Kneap)

N

Traigh na Beirigh
(Berie Sands)

Riof
(Reef)

Walk 8

1 km

1 mile

1 Stroll on down the narrow road to the small pier. Turn right to walk south-east across the sandy bay, which is sheltered by the islands of Pabbay (Pabaigh) and Shiaram (Siaram). Here you might see ringed plover and dunlin racing over the beach after sand flies. If the tide is high you may have to walk the shore road, which you join, from the beach, just before the last two dwellings.

2 After passing the last house, turn left to climb the cliff, keeping to the right of the fence. Here on the cliff top, in summer, a magnificent carpet of flowers delights the eye. Look for deep purple orchis, harebells, lady's bedstraw, field gentians, self heal, hayrattle, frog orchid and meadow rue. Continue along the cliff edge, keeping beside the fence.

3 Descend the slopes to reach the extensive silver sands of Berie, which are protected from the Atlantic rollers by the island of Vacsay (Bhacsaigh). Press on ahead to the towering rock of the cliff at the end of the wonderful sands and climb right to a stile over a fence. Walk up the slope and bear left to look across Loch Roag (Rog) to the island of Vuia Mor, with Great Bernera (Bearnaraigh) beyond. Head on round the cliff. Pass a tiny bay where the water turns to aquamarine over the sand. Carry on along the cliffs and climb through a damper gully, where sundew, cotton-grass and marsh lousewort flourish. Follow the cliffs round, always keeping the sea loch to the left, until you reach a fence.

Field Gentian

34

4 Pass through the gate in line with a dwelling. Bear slightly left to a second gate and then right to a third gate to the start of a narrow road to Reef (Riof). Walk the road with Loch Linish (Lionais) to your right. Turn right at the T-junction and stroll on, soon leaving the dwellings behind. Enjoy the lonely road, which passes through rocky outcrops. Continue to the sands of Berie. Here you may wish to continue on the road to rejoin your car, or you may be tempted to walk the sands and the cliff before returning to the road at the start of Kneep.

Heron

Practicals

Type of walk: Generally easy walking over superb sandy beaches or along breezy cliffs, with fine views to be enjoyed.

Distance: 5 miles / 8km
Time: 3 hours
Maps: OS Explorer 458 / Landranger 13

9

Beehive dwellings below Scalaval (Scalabhal) Hill, Lewis

Park at the end of the minor road on the west side of the bridge by the head of Little Loch Roag (Loch Rog Beag), at grid ref. 139237. To access this leave Stornoway by the A859, signposted Tarbert. Take the right turn in Liurbost towards Callanish and Carloway for the A858, then turn left onto the B8011 at Garynahine (Gearraidh na h-Aibhne). Shortly after the bridge over the head of Loch Rog Beag, where the road swings north, take the minor road on the left and continue to the road end.

No one seems to know exactly what the **ancient beehive-shaped structures** at grid ref. 132200, the aim of this walk, were used for. A local man suggested that they might have been temporary homes for people at the shielings. They are situated in a pleasing hollow close to a feeder stream that joins the Abhainn a' Loin below the rocky slopes of Scalaval.

Beehive hut, Scalabhal

1 Cross the road and go through the gate, which carries a notice that says it is a private road but walkers are welcome. No dogs are allowed. Walk the access track towards Morsgail Lodge (Loidse Mhorsgail), a reinforced way that runs beside a hurrying peat-stained burn, a favourite haunt of herons. The track passes first through moorland and then scattered rhododendrons and gorse. Continue on between alders, birch, willow and conifers, a welcome relief from the addictive but bleak Lewis scenery. The track curves gracefully and Morsgail Lodge lies ahead.

2 Carry on for just over a mile from the start and then bear left, over a bridge, which crosses the burn just below the weir at the foot of Loch Morsgail. Carry on beside the loch where the peaty track can be very muddy in places. It has been reinforced with old tyres, for the use of 'argos', 8-wheeled cross country vehicles used during stalking. Continue to the head of the loch and pass through a ricketty gate close to the wind-rippled water. Cross a small stream on a stone slab and the walk on round the head of the loch until you come to the bridge over the Abhainn a' Loin.

Bog Asphodel and Sphagnum

Walk 9

Loch Rog Beag
(Little Loch Roag)
B8011

N

Morsgail Lodge

Loch Morsgail

Scalabhal
(Scalaval)

1km
1 mile

beehives

37

3 Do NOT cross but continue upstream (there is no higher bridge, as labelled on the OS map, and the river is not easy to re-cross). There is no real path up this east bank of the river. The easiest going is fairly close to the burn although you have to skirt a large boggy area shortly before joining the track coming in on your right. This can be really muddy and churned up in places due to the use of argos along it. Carry on along the track for nearly a mile as it winds on, with the rocky slopes of Scalaval to your left, to reach the beehive dwellings (132200), which stand just where the track drops down to a stream. Pause here to explore the lonely little site. In clear weather there are lovely views, south, to Sron Ulladale (walk 17). As you go look out for golden plovers on the moors and listen for their plaintive calls. To return, retrace your outward route.

Golden Plover

Practicals

Type of walk: There is a metalled road for a third of the way and then the walk continues over moorland on indistinct paths and tracks that can be very muddy. Do not be put off by the mud as this can be a very enjoyable walk and the beehives are fascinating and are really worth the effort of getting to them.

Distance: 6 miles / 9.8km
Time: 3 hours
Maps: OS Explorer 458 / Landranger 13

10

Uig Sands
(Traigh Uige), Lewis

(Walkers, please remember to check on the tides)

Park beyond the gates at the end of the road, close to the toilets, grid ref. 049329. To reach this, leave Stornoway by the A858. Turn left at Garynahine (Gearraidh na h-Aibhne) onto the B8011 and continue alongside Little Loch Roag. Follow the road through Glen Valtos (Gleann Bhaltois) and on through the settlement of Ardroil (Eadar Dha Fhadhail). Beyond, the road to the shore is well signposted.

The Lewis chessmen, carved from walrus ivory, were found in a sandbank at Uig in 1831. Seventy pieces were found belonging to several incomplete sets, believed to have been carved around 1050 and were probably made in Scandinavia. The glum bishops, brooding queens and soldiers biting the edges of their shields in an

Bridge, Uig Sands

ecstasy of rage or dread are regarded as among the British Museum's greatest treasures. Eleven more are owned by the Museum of Scotland. Copies can be seen in the Francis Street Museum, Stornoway.

Legend says they were buried many years before by the murderer of a sailor lad who had brought them ashore from a passing ship. Some believe they were the stock of a travelling ivory salesman.

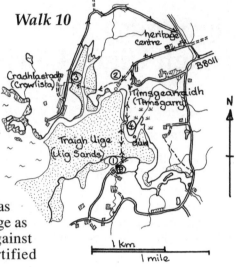

Walk 10

Dun Borranish (Borranais), which you may wish to visit, was built in the early Iron Age as a communal refuge against invaders and as a fortified look-out post.

Arthur Ransome, the author of *Swallows and Amazons*, stayed at Uig Lodge, overlooking the sands. He was suffering from writer's block and was encouraged by his friend, Myles North, to use the Lodge as a retreat and a place to recuperate. Here he was inspired to write his last novel, *Great Northern Diver?*

1 Walk down the track from the parking area, pass through the sand dunes and continue on across the great expanse of hour-glass fine, silvery sand. As you go, look right to see the green hill on which stands Uig Lodge. Stroll slightly left across the lovely sands towards a sturdy bridge, difficult to spot up against the cliffs, opposite. It was built in 1980 to span a hurrying burn. Once across, walk up the slope and bear left across short-cropped turf, where harebells bloom and wheatears flit among the rocks in late summer. Continue along the shore and turn right to pass to the left of a small cottage. Stride on along the access track, turn left at the end and walk to a triangular green. Here turn left to walk a narrow road, towards a guesthouse, once the manse and a listed building.

40

2 Keep to the right of the old manse and walk the grassy sward. Pause here to look at the old burial ground of Baile na Cille. Beyond stretch the sands, with the hills of West Lewis providing a dramatic backcloth. Stride on, descending an ancient grassy fenced track to the shore. Then go on across the sands, finding the easiest way across the stream bed to arrive by a gate on the opposite shore in front of a dwelling, closest to the sands, at Crowlista (Cradhlastadh).

3 Turn right and walk the narrow road above the lovely bay, where in summer primroses flower and green plovers strut regally across the moorland. Climb the slope and continue to where the road curves right towards Timsgarry (Timsgearraidh). At the T-junction, turn right, and carry on to take the next right turn. Stride past a dwelling and the school. Immediately adjacent to the latter is the flourishing heritage centre. It has a good cafe, serving homebaking. Go on to pass the church. At the triangle of grass passed earlier, turn left. Walk to the cottage and bear left beyond. Then go on over the sandy turf to the bridge.

4 Before you cross, walk on to go over a rocky causeway at the end of the small cliffs. This leads to the last tiny hillock and the faint remains of Dun Borranish. In summer the sward around is one mass of pink thrift. Return to cross the bridge, and as you dawdle over the sands, think of the sailor lad murdered long ago. Walk the cart track through the dunes and over the turf to return to the parking area.

Lapwing

Practicals

Type of walk: A lovely walk, over glorious sands. Boots essential if you wish to cross the river channel dryshod.

Distance: 5 ½ miles / 9km
Time: 3 hours
Maps: OS Explorer 458 / Landranger 13

Always check on the tides

11

Loch Langavat (Langabhat), Lewis

Park close to Aline Lodge (Loidse Ath Linne), grid ref. 197119. This is reached by taking the A859 south from Stornoway. Just before the access road to the dwelling on the shore, there is a small parking area on the right, approached by a rough track.

Shieling is the name given to using summer pastures for feeding livestock. Arable land in Lewis is scarce and crofters were compelled to exploit grazing on the surrounding moorland. Fodder obtained from the pastures near to the settlements was conserved for winter use. On this walk the remains of scattered shieling huts are visited. These were temporary homes, mainly for women and children who spent the summer, often remote from their communities, tending the animals.

*Waterfall on
Abhainn a' Mhuil*

Walk 11

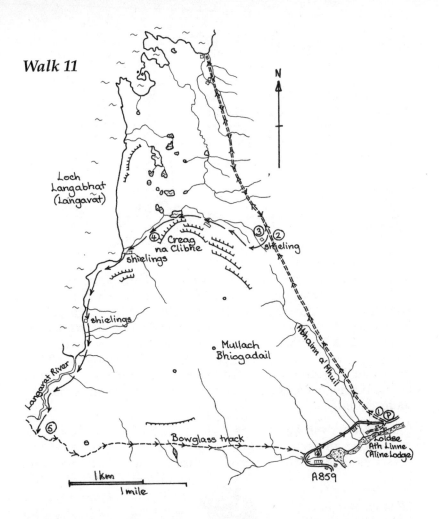

1 Walk inland up the reinforced track, climbing steadily. Look back often to enjoy the glorious view along Loch Seaforth (Shiphoirt) and out to sea. Moorland stretches away on both sides of the track, and where the way has been maintained you can see how thick the peat can be ranging from two to eight feet. Watch out for buzzards overhead and stags high on the tops. Look for the cascading waterfall on the Abhainn a' Mhuil and walk on until you can see the ruins of a shieling away to the left (about 2 miles from the start).

2 Here a decision has to be made. Energetic walkers will wish to continue on along the track for another 1 ½ miles. As the track descends gently to the shore of Loch Langavat, look for the ruins of more shielings. If the weather is kind you will want to linger on the shores of this large mountain-girt loch.

Butterwort

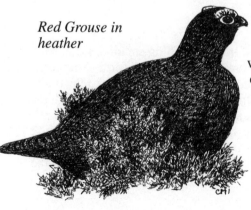

3 Then return along the 1 ½ miles until you can see the shieling, viewed earlier, and now on your right. Here a second decision needs to be made. Some walkers will wish to return along the track to the parking area near Aline Lodge. For those who want a more adventurous route and are strong walkers, unperturbed by a trackless and often wet moorland, they should leave the track here, south, and make their way to the shieling. Then go on over some rather wet heather moorland and across a tributary of the Clibhe burn. Climb a little way up the lower slopes of Creag na Clibhe before bearing right (north-west) to arrive at the scant remains of more shielings.

4 Then contour on, keeping as high as is comfortable, below the steep slopes of Creag na Clibhe, follow the Clibhe burn down to a grassy hollow on the shore of the loch, where there are more shielings. Continue south below the steep slopes of Cleit Earscleit, stepping across hurrying streams and watching out for red grouse on the heathery slopes. When you are about parallel with the southern end of the magnificent loch you come to the side of the wide Langavat River, which your follow upstream. To your right, look for the east-west

Red Grouse in heather

track, the Bowglass track, crossing the northern slopes of Stulaval (Stuabhal).

5 Join this track at approximately grid ref. 148120, turning left to climb the zig-zag route. Ascend steadily to the cairn at the head of the pass, Bealach na h-Uamha. Once over the top, the houses by Loch Seaforth come into view, two miles downhill. At the end of the track, turn left and walk the A859 to return to the parking place.

Merganser with ducklings

Practicals

Type of walk: The circular walk takes you along two tracks linked by a 3 mile stretch of pathless moorland from where there are superb views of Lewis's wild remote hills and lonely lochs. The linear route gives a much easier walk to a fine loch. Suitable for seasoned fell walkers.

Distance:	From Aline Lodge to Loch Langavat, returning by the Bowglass track 11 ½ miles / 19km. Leaving the outward track at the shieling and returning by the Bowglass track 8 miles / 13km. Linear walk from Aline Lodge to Loch Langavat 7 miles / 11.4km
Time:	6–7 hours; 4–5 hours; 3–4 hours
Maps:	OS Explorer 456 / Landranger 13

12

St Columba's Church (Eaglais na h-Aoidhe), Aiginish (Aiginis), and Tiumpan Head (Rubha an t-Siumpain), Lewis

To visit St Columba's church, Aiginish, park in the car park, where there are toilets, grid ref. 478323. There is also an alternative parking place at grid ref. 484321. To reach this, leave Stornoway by the A866 to cross the thin strip of land that links the Eye peninsula, with the rest of Lewis.

The **ruined church** is one of the most important religious sites on Lewis. It is dedicated to St Columba, who arrived from Iona in AD 563. The church was built on the site of a cell occupied by the Celtic saint, Catan, in the seventh century. It is believed that 19 chiefs of the MacLeods of Lewis are buried here. At the time of writing the church is unsafe and entry to the building is no longer permitted. It may be going to be repaired in the future but is unclear if or when.

Lighthouse, Tiumpan Head

Located close to St Columba's church is the award-winning project, built in 1996, that commemorates the **Highland Land Raiders**.

If the tide is low you can walk the **golden sands**, west of St Columba's. From here, in summer, you might spot vast numbers of terns congregating on the island of Langa Sgeir Mhor and Manx shearwaters skimming above the waves offshore. There are also good views across the Broad Bay to the rugged eastern coastline of Lewis. The access road that crosses the isthmus is protected from the huge waves of the Minch by strong sea walls.

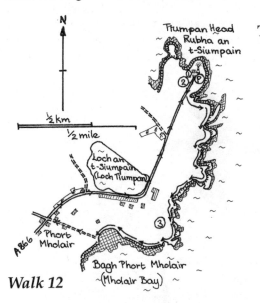

The **lighthouse at Tiumpan Head** was built in 1900 after a request was made for a watch to be kept on illegal activities out at sea. In 1956 the then seven years old Prince Charles sounded the newly installed fog siren.

Walk 12

1 After your visit to St Columba's (cemetery only alas), drive on along the A866 for a further six miles; where the A-road makes a sharp turn left, proceed ahead to the car park at Tiumpan Head lighthouse, grid ref. 575378. From here enjoy the magnificent view across the Minch to mainland Scotland. Look, in summer, for the large colonies of fulmars and kittiwakes that nest on the huge cliffs and stacks. Basking sharks and whales can sometimes be seen.

2 Then stroll back along the road for 50 yards and walk left over the grassy cliffs. Enjoy the heather and scabious-covered turf and with

the Minch now to your left. Follow the indented coastline, with care, always moving inland if you feel too close to the edge. Huge rock faces slope down to the sea, the upper parts coloured by brilliant orange lichen. In the wetter areas, look on the turf for sundew, orchis and lousewort. As you go you should see gannets dive for fish in the Minch and terns fly overhead.

3 Continue on along the cliffs and also where they curve round right at the start of Mholair Bay until you can join a narrow road. Bear right to walk inland and carry on until you reach the crossroads. Then walk right again along the road to the lighthouse. Go past a rare planting of trees and then on to the side of Loch Tiumpan (Loch an t-Siumpain), where you will want to dawdle for more bird-watching. Then stride on along the road, past more woodland and then out onto the moorland to come to the parking area at the lighthouse.

Manx Shearwaters

Practicals

Type of walk: Easy walking all the way and mainly dry.
Wonderful sea views.

Distance:	3 miles / 5km
Time:	1 ½ hours. Add on the time spent at St Columba's and on the beach.
Maps:	OS Explorer 459 / Landranger 8

13

Tolsta Head
(Ceann Tholastaidh), Lewis

Park in the car park for Traigh Mhor, grid ref. 534493. To reach this, leave Stornoway by the A857 and turn right at Newmarket onto the B895. Drive through Tunga, Col, Bac, Griais, and North Tolsta. Continue through New Tolsta, crossing the cattle grid and driving on to take the next narrow right turn that descends to the small parking area, on the edge of the magnificent bay.

Traigh Ghioradail

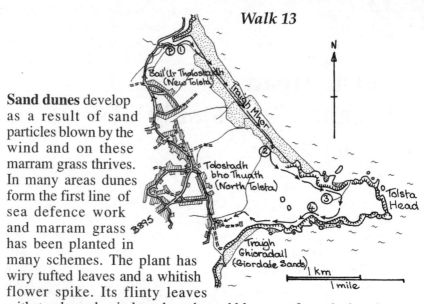

Walk 13

N

Sand dunes develop as a result of sand particles blown by the wind and on these marram grass thrives. In many areas dunes form the first line of sea defence work and marram grass has been planted in many schemes. The plant has wiry tufted leaves and a whitish flower spike. Its flinty leaves withstand rough winds and catch sand blown up from the beaches so that it collects in hummocks around them, all helping the sand hills to become stabilised.

1 Leave the car park by the stile and cross, by footbridge, the foaming cascades of the Allt na Muilne. Walk on over the sands of the river's outlet and bear right along the immense golden strand. Dunes, held firm by flowering marram grass, rise up on the landward side and close to these the lilac flowers of sea rocket thrive. Continue on and on, watching for gannets and in the distance you might spot the mountains of the mainland.

2 Carry on until you have passed Tolsta cemetery, on slopes to the right, and have stepped over three narrow, shallow streams hurrying across the sands to the sea. Then head inland to climb shallow cliffs beyond the last stream, swinging left to ascend to the top of the huge cliffs that lead to Tolsta Head. Here, in summer, the turf is one mass of colour, with eyebright, buttercup, hawkweed, pignut, red clover, lady's bedstraw, kidney vetch, scabious, field gentian, ragwort and yarrow.

3 When you reach the fence that crosses the headland from inland to the cliff edge, head right to pass through a gate and then return to nearer the cliff edge. Walk with care along the top of the cliffs, keeping a safe and comfortable distance from the edge. Here the sward changes and the rough grass is sparsely carpeted with few moorland flowers. Listen as you go for the soft cooing of the fulmars, which nest in huge numbers using every available ledge on the cliffs.

4 Wind on round Tolsta Head with, across Broad Bay, Tiumpan lighthouse, on the Eye Peninsula, coming into view. Walk on along the cliffs to look down on several natural arches and then look ahead to see the small pier jutting into the silvery Giordale (Ghioradail) Sands. Beyond, you might spot a pencil-slim waterfall descending the cliff. On reaching a fence, walk inland beside it. Follow it until you come to a gap where there is a faint vehicle track cutting off left towards the village. This leads up a section of rough grazing and brings you to a gate onto a track; turn right and follow the track round until you reach the road in North Tolsta (Tolastadh bho Thuath). At the B-road, turn right and continue through New Tolsta (Bail' Ur Tholastaidh) to return to the car park.

Gannet diving

Practicals

Type of walk: Time your walk for when the tide is out and then you can stroll the 1 ½ miles of silvery sand and perhaps leave the only footsteps to be seen. On the steady climb to the cliff top and then on round the Head, you should proceed with care. Some road walking.

Distance: 6 ½ miles / 10.6km
Time: 3–4 hours
Maps: OS Explorer 460 / Landranger 8

14

Traigh Ghearadha, Tolsta (Tolastadh), to Skigersta (Sgiogarstaigh), Ness (Nis), Lewis

Park at Garry Bay (Traigh Ghearadha), grid ref. 533499. To access this use the same approach route as for walk 13 and continue past the Traigh Mhor (Long Beach) parking area, to turn right at the signpost for the next car park.

Before you reach the turn off for the parking area you might be tempted to park on the side of the road, above **Garry Bay** and look down on the fine sea stacks, grass covered pillars of rock that have become separated from the main cliffs. These large stacks hide small caves and tunnels. The largest in the bay supports the remains of Caisteal a'Mhorair, Mormaer's Castle. It was built after Norway's cession of the Hebrides to Scotland in 1266 when Lewis became part of the Earldom of Ross.

Bridge to Nowhere

This linear walk is 10 miles long. It takes you from the lushness of the surrounds of the Garry River, over way-marked lonely moorland, with superb coastal scenery, to a track that starts at Filiscleitir and carries on to the road at Skigersta, Ness. **Some careful planning needs to go into the expedition.** If two cars are available, one can be left at either end but the two car parks are many miles apart by road. Or you could do half the walk one day returning to the parking area and then start from the other end and complete the other half another day. Or you may wish to spend the time available, exploring the lovely Traigh Ghearadha and then crossing the 'Bridge to Nowhere' before descending the far side of the river to view the waterfall. For information on useful buses, telephone the bus station at Stornoway, 01851 704327.

The handsome **'Bridge to Nowhere'** spans the Garry River (Abhainn Ghearadha). It was built by Lord Leverhulme for a road he intended to run to Ness. He had bought the island of Lewis in 1918 and hoped to improve the island's economy by making the remoter parts of the island more accessible and provide employment. Alas the road was never built because of trouble with the soldiers returning from the war and the escalating costs of the development work. The fine bridge is a poignant memorial to Lord Leverhume's failed dream.

Walk 14

53

1 From the parking area, return to the road and turn right to cross the bridge. Here the tarmac ceases and a way-marked reinforced track continues. Follow it as it winds round a headland from where you have fine views of the Garry Beach and the Long Beach, with Tolsta Head beyond. Carry on along the track until it peters out at a concrete slab over the Abhainn na Cloich. Here some walkers will wish to turn right and follow a narrow path over the heather moorland to the side of the falls on the tempestuous river before returning to the parking area by their outward route.

Fulmar

2 To continue the walk, carry on along the main way for a short distance and, where the track turns away left, head for a way-mark on a hillock ahead. At this point you may wish to move right to the cliff edge to see Dun Othail, a sea stack almost severed from the mainland by a deep ravine, known as MacNicol's Leap. Legend has it that MacNicol was castrated by a MacLeod chief. In revenge MacNicol kidnapped the chief's only son and retreated to Dun Othail. He refused to return the child unless his father went through similar castration. Once MacNicol was assured this had happened, he leapt to his death into the chasm carrying the boy, yelling as he went 'I will not have an heir and neither shall you!'

3 Carry on along the edge of the cliffs on a trod made by other walkers or on animal tracks for about 2 miles to come to Cuilatotar. Here look for a lonely ruined house, once the home of John MacDonald. He had been press-ganged into the navy. When he was released and returned to Lewis he found there was no land for him. So he settled here where he could find peace and lots of space. He chose well, with great views down to the sea.

4 At Cuilatotar, the main route swings inland, so avoiding the deep Diobadal ravine and this might be the point at which some walkers will wish to return. For those with transport at the other end, follow the way-marks taking you by the easiest route across the boggy ground to pass the ruins of summer shielings. The route then continues on over heather moorland, wet in places, with the steep cliffs of the east coast to your right.

5 After another two miles the old shieling village, Filiscleitir, is reached. These summer dwellings were used by the people of Lionel (Lional) in Ness although most of what remains now is a grass-grown mound of clustered ruins. The three ruined buildings along the cliff top repay a visit. The southernmost is the remains of a small chapel built by John Nicolson of Lional, once a Baptist preacher in America, to serve the people from the shielings. Today the little chapel lies silent. The northernmost ruin is the remains of John Nicolson's house, built on the old Dun Filiscleitir. From the cliffs here you may be rewarded with a view down to a fine double natural arch. Watch out for great skuas, as well as fulmars and kittiwakes, which nest on the cliffs. From John Nicolson's house, follow the cliffs round a short distance before turning inland to cross the old peat workings to reach the ruined shieling village.

Black Guillemot

6 Once past Filiscleitir you join a track, initially muddy but gradually improving as you move north. After about three quarters of a mile you reach Cuidhsiadar, a scattered settlement of shielings along the valley of the Abhainn Dubh used by the people from Ness since 1877. Whilst many of these are ruins, some are still maintained as summer retreats by crofters. Continue along the good vehicle track, which passes through active peat workings. Look out for buzzards and kestrels hunting over the moors, and you may be lucky enough to get a rare view of a sea eagle. After a mile or so you reach the surfaced road and the parking area south of Skigersta.

Practicals

Type of walk: Challenging. Seasoned walkers will enjoy this exacting walk over rolling (and boggy) moorland, with superb coastal scenery. You might spot an eagle or a peregrine, both nest along this coastline. Out to sea you should see both common and grey seals and, maybe, a school of dolphins.

Distance: 10 miles / 16km
Time: 5–6 hours
Maps: OS Explorer 460 / Landranger 8

15

Clisham (An Cliseam),
Harris (Na Hearadh)

Park near the bridge over the Scaladale River (Abhainn Scaladail) at grid ref. 183099. To reach this, drive south from Stornoway or north from Tarbert on the A859.

Walk the dramatic **Clisham ridge**, the highest hill in the Western Isles. From the summit you look down to deep blue sea lochs and small hill lochs tucked into hollows in the wild slopes. It is a landscape that seems more likely to be Iceland. Watch out as you go for golden eagles and buzzards overhead (or below if on the summit). Look too for magical sightings of deer on the surrounding tops.

1 Set off (south) down the A859 for about 550 yds / 500m until you reach a good track on the right, at grid reference 186096.

Clisham & Tomnabhal, Loch Mhisteam

Walk 15

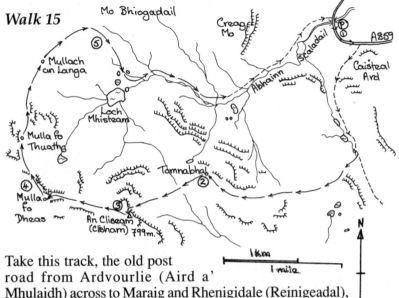

Take this track, the old post
road from Ardvourlie (Aird a'
Mhulaidh) across to Maraig and Rhenigidale (Reinigeadal),
and walk along it as it leads you up the hillside above the
Scaladale River. Follow the track as it bends left, passing
two small lochans. As it reaches the highest point, bear off to your
right and climb up the steep grassy slope. Continue across the moor
towards Tomnaval (Tomnabhal), aiming for the gentler slope at
the south-eastern end. Here turn right to follow the crest of
Tomnaval towards the corrie until you reach the summit cairn (1815
ft / 552m) from where you have a splendid view across North Harris.

2 Bear left to look across to a col and the north east slope of Clisham.
 Head down to the col, aiming for the highest point, then begin to
 climb up the steep side of Clisham by bearing slightly to your right
 to avoid the worst of the boulder fields before heading straight up
 to a grassy ramp leading diagonally right through crags. As you
 near the crags, look out for a small footpath, which starts to lead
 up this ramp but then turns and heads straight up to a gap in the
 crags on the skyline. Follow the path, turning left with it to reach
 the summit ridge above the cliff line. The trig point (2597 ft / 799m)
 is surrounded by a circular wall as a shelter, which can be entered
 by climbing over it carefully.

3 Pause here to admire the views across Harris and Lewis. Then make
 for the narrow ridge joining Clisham with the next peak, Mulla Fo

57

Dheas (2530 ft / 743m). As you go, pick a careful route through the boulders until you reach a more grassy area with an indistinct path. This leads you down to a narrow col and then on up the narrow, rocky ridge over the intermediate peak of An t-Isean. Follow the path round and then make your way on along one of the several paths that take you up the ridge to gain the summit. Look out for starry saxifrage growing between the rocks and mountain hares hurrying along the ridges.

Mountain Hare

4 The footpath continues along the obvious ridge towards Mulla Fo Thuath (2366 ft / 720m), descending a col before climbing again to the summit. From here follow the path on across the much wider ridge. Take care to keep left to avoid the cliffs. Continue along the ridge crest as you ascend Mullach an Langa (2000 ft / 614m) which is a much wider peak, rocky rather than craggy. Pause to admire the views a last time, then head down the steep grassy slope. Look out for red deer crossing the moorland as you descend the hill.

5 As you reach the bottom of the steep section of this hill, bear to your right towards Loch Mhisteam across the old moraine deposits. Here you are likely to see golden plover and to hear their plaintive calls warning of predators. Do NOT cross the river, but turn left to follow it downstream, keeping to animal tracks where possible. The river brings you gradually down the corrie, under the impressive cliffs of Creag Mo to your left, where the footpath become clearer and more well-trodden. Continue down the path until you regain the A859 beside the bridge over the Scaladale River, and your car.

Practicals

Type of walk: A challenging mountain climb for experienced hill walkers. Check the weather reports before you start out and be prepared to turn back if the weather deteriorates. Good footwear essential.

Distance: 9 miles / 14.5km
Time: 7–8 hours for experienced walkers in good weather
Maps: OS Explorer 456 / Landranger 13

16

Hushinish (Huisinis), Harris

Park in the car park by the toilets, grid ref. 993121, above the lovely sandy beach at Hushinish. To reach this leave Tarbert (Tairbeart), north, by the A859 and after 2 miles take the B887, left. This follows a twisting route along the northern shores of West Loch Tarbert.

A mile along the B-road, find a suitable place to park and look at the chimney of **an old whaling station at Bunavoneadar** (Bun Abhainn Eadar). The station was established before the 1914–18 war by Norwegians. In 1922 Lord Leverhulme, after he had purchased North Harris, bought out the Norwegian interest in the station, but by 1930 the venture had proved a failure.

Continue along the narrow road to park just before the white gates of Abhainn Suidhe Castle. Walk on to see the superb falls on the burn that descends from Loch Leosaid. Where the white-topped water enters the sea-loch, Loch Leosavay, **salmon congregate** in vast numbers, their fins parting the water like mini-sharks. Regularly, a large fish makes a leap into the air and then another before it begins the seemingly perilous ascent to spawn.

Sound of Scarp,
Hushinish

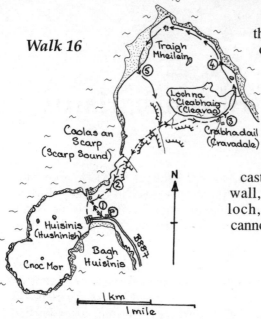

Walk 16

Traigh Mheilein

Loch na Cleabhaig (Cleavag)

Crabhadail (Cravadale)

Caolas an Scarp (Scarp Sound)

Huisinis (Hushinish)

Cnoc Mor

Bagh Huisinis

N

1 km
1 mile

A short distance along the road you pass in front of the **castle**. This was built by the Earl of Dunmore in 1868 and it was the Countess, his wife, who restored St Clement's church at Rodel (walk 19). A wide lawn fronts the castle and in a castellated wall, overlooking the sea-loch, stand several small cannon.

1 Park on a long narrow lay-by above the beach and take a single-track sandy road that leads off north. In summer it is bordered with buttercups and very large deep blue harebells and leads to a little pier where small boats leave to go to the island of Scarp. Just before the pier, take a track that leads right across a glorious stretch of machair. Pass through a gate and walk on along a narrow path to a stile over a long wall.

2 Follow the wide, well-made track as it climbs up and up high above the rocky shore. Where the track ceases, continue along a narrow path that goes on to swing right. Follow it as it climbs through a narrow corridor between two hills. At the top of the gully, first the sea loch, Loch Cravadale (Crabhadail), comes into view and then Loch na Cleavag (Loch na Cleabhaig), a freshwater loch. The indistinct path hugs the base of the steep side of Husival Beag (Huiseabhal Beag) on the right. Here, out of reach of hungry

Centaury

sheep, honeysuckle blossoms.

3 The way continues along the shore of Loch na Cleavag to come to a crofthouse. Pause in this quiet hollow where you might see a golden eagle making use of rising thermals. Stroll on around Loch na Cleavag and cross the narrow strip of land between it and the sea where the pounding waves have thrown up a huge barrier of rounded boulders. From these look right (east) into Glen Cravadale, a forbidding U-shaped valley with sheer sides, softened by its reflections in Loch a' Ghlinne.

4 Walk on to the next great barrier of boulders and then look across to Loch Resort (Reasort), which is shadowed by high hills on both sides. This deep, narrow sea inlet forms the boundary between Harris and Lewis. Stride on along the shallow grassy cliffs, with the sea to your right, crossing a vast area of lazybeds, where the pretty centaury grows. Carry on around the cliffs until you reach the wonderful extensive sands of Traigh Mheilein, which is bordered by high dunes on your left.

5 From the sands look across Scarp Sound to Scarp itself to see how many old dwelling you can count. Perhaps you can make out the ruined school and perhaps the church. Stroll to the end of the sands and then strike inland, heading steadily up towards the path taken earlier at the start of the gully. Follow the path, later a track, to retrace your outward route.

Ravens

Practicals

Type of walk: An exhilarating walk through a lovely remote part of Harris. Generally easy walking. Cliff path a little vertiginous in one part. Gully path can be wet. Boulder walking is quite hard going. Machair and sands glorious.

Distance: 5 miles / 8km
Time: 3 hours
Maps: OS Explorer 456 / Landranger 13

17

Glen Chliostair and Sron Ulladale (Sron Uladal), Harris

Park carefully by the cattle grid near Abhainn Suidhe Castle, grid ref. 052078. Please obey the 'no parking' signs in the passing places down towards the castle. To access the parking area, take the A859 north from Tarbert and turn left along the B887.

On this walk keep a look out for **red deer**. The stalking season is from Aug. 12 to Oct. 12 and visitors are advised to exercise care during this period. The deer tend to keep to the high ground during the summer. A fully grown stag stands up to 1.4m at the shoulder, the hind somewhat less. The summer coat is reddish-brown, sometimes golden-red and changes to brownish-grey in winter with the new growth of grey hairs. A patch of white

Sron Ulladale

around the short tail furnishes a recognition mark, common to most of the deer family, which possibly serves as a guide to other members of the herd when in flight from a predator.

1 Take the narrow road, north from the B887, signposted to Chliostair power station. Once on the access road look back to see the culverts that allow the outlet burn from Lochan Beag to pass under the road, some modern and some much older. Follow the road past Lochan Beag, taking the left branch after the loch to pass the gate welcoming you to the North Harris estate. After a short distance Loch Leosaid comes into view on your right, with a splendid waterfall at the top of the outflow burn. Here you might be lucky to see a pair of red-throated divers.

2 Press on, following the track as it winds round the loch, crossing the River Leosaid and past the small power station. Walk on up the valley beside the pipeline to reach the unusual arched dam and the reservoir, Loch Chliostair, behind it. From the dam a well-made stalkers' path heads along the right shore of the loch then leads off up Gleann Chliostair towards Loch Ashavat (Aiseabhat) just below the col.

3 Continue round to the left of Loch Ashavat and over the col to get your first view of Sron Ulladale with its towering cliffs. Follow the footpath as it follows the Ulladale River down the valley, bringing more of the spectacular 250m-high cliffs into view. This is a favourite haunt of rock climbers with its long routes and challenging overhangs. The path continues round below Sron Ulladale, bringing you to the shores of Loch Ulladale from where

Loch Uladal (Ulladale)

Sron Uladal (Ulladale)

Loch Aiseabhat (Ashavat)

Loch Chliostair

dam

power station

Loch Leosaid

Lochan Beag

B887

Walk 17

N

1 km

1 mile

there are excellent views back to the main buttresses as well as down the valley towards Reasort and South Lewis.

4 Return by the same route and enjoy the fine views of the indented coastline and the islands that lie below you. If you failed to see the salmon leaping from pool to pool on the cascades tumbling over rocks, described in walk 16, you might wish to carry on towards the castle and end this walk in this way.

Red Deer Stag

Practicals

Type of walk: This is a serious hill walk, with dramatic scenery. Walk as far as you feel happy and then return by the same route.

Distance:	5 miles each way / 16km in all.
Time:	6 hours
Maps:	OS Explorer 456 / Landranger 13

18

Chaipaval (Ceapabhal), South Harris

Park near the unmanned visitor centre, beyond Northton (Taobh Tuath), where there are toilets, grid ref. 989904. To access this leave Tarbert, south, on the A859. Pass through some very rocky terrain and then drive on along the lovely coast to take the sharp right turn for Northton.

On your drive along the A-road towards Northton, you might like to park at the south end of the beach, grid ref. 038966, close to Horgabost. From this parking area walk across the sands and climb the hill to reach the **Horgabost standing stone** and enjoy the delightful view across to the island of Taransay (Tarasaigh), used for the TV Castaway series.

South Harris from Chaipaval

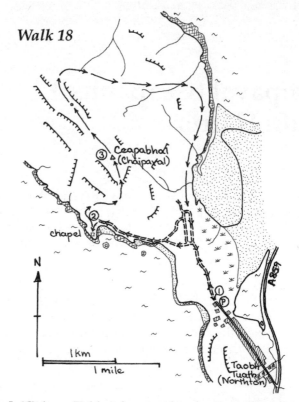

Walk 18

Toe Head (Gob an Tobha) is a peninsula extending some three miles out into the Atlantic in the south-west corner of Harris. It is joined to Northton by a narrow strand of machair with sandy beaches on each side, and is capped by the hill of Chaipaval. This hill rises to a height of 1092 ft / 368m and provides a splendid grandstand to view the islands in the Sound of Harris and on a clear day it is possible to see St Kilda to the west.

Early on in this walk you reach a small eminence on which stands a roofless ruin, its lichen encrusted walls, standing tall. This is **Rubh' an Teampuill**, thought to have been built in the early sixteenth century, about the time of St Clement's at Rodel (visited on walk 19).

Hen Harrier

66

1 Walk on from the parking area along the continuing sandy track and where this branches take the left fork. This leads you over glorious machair, with good views of the sands on the west side of the isthmus. Stride on through a gate and continue along the clear track above the lovely coastline in the direction of the ruin, where you will want to pause.

2 Then head on along the way across the machair to a stile in the wall. Beyond, turn right to begin the long, stiff climb towards the summit of Chaipaval, steadily bearing right, through a magnificent rockery of heather that continues for a thousand feet. On the flattish top of the hill a good path continues through a peaty wasteland, first to the triangulation point and then to the summit cairn.

3 Enjoy the wonderful views in all directions and the many islands scattered around the skirts of Harris. On a good day you might spot the Skye Cuillin to the south-east and also St Kilda, to the west. To return, descend by your outward route or, follow the contours round the north-east side of the hill, a challenging steady drop through the heather moorland to a gate in the fence. From here, walk down through the machair to pick up one of the several tracks leading right to the parking area.

Heather

C.M. Isherwood

Practicals

Type of walk: The route to the ruin is sheer delight. Stiff scramble to the summit whichever way you choose—seasoned walkers will enjoy the challenge.

Distance: 5 ½ miles / 9km
Time: 3–4 hours
Maps: OS Explorer 455 / Landranger 18

19

Rodel (Roghadal), South Harris

Park close to St Clement's church, Rodel, grid ref. 048832. To reach this, take the A859 to its end at the southern tip of Harris.

The church dates from the first decades of the sixteenth century and, after various vicissitudes was restored to its present state by the Countess of Dunmore in 1873. Climb the slope to the church, to see the austere, stunning interior and perhaps to climb its sturdy tower (built on a rocky outcrop) for a magnificent view. Thought to have been built by the MacLeods of Dunvegan (Skye), the church was the family's traditional burial place and there are three MacLeod tombs. The principal one is of **the chief, Alasdair Crotach MacLeod**. It was constructed by him in 1528, 20 years before his death. The tomb is set in a recessed arch in the south wall, and the tombstone depicts a knight in armour carved in local black Gneiss rock. The recess is elaborately carved and shows the 12 apostles, a pair of angels and the

St. Clement's Church, Rodel

Holy Trinity. In a small walled enclosure in the churchyard are the tombs of the MacDonalds and more MacLeods.

1 Walk back (north) along the A-road to take a reinforced track on the left (west). Follow it as it runs beside a picturesque loch where amphibious bistort flowers. Cross a wooden bridge over the exit stream that flows into the sea loch, Loch Rodel. Stride ahead from the bridge to walk a wide grassy track until you reach a fence, then follow it right and climb the flower-bedecked low cliff overlooking the loch. From here you have a good view over the islands in the Sound of Harris. Pass through a gate and continue on the pleasing path. The way then drops down and swings left and passes through another gate. Press on further and cross an access track to a house, and then on to reach a metalled road where you turn left.

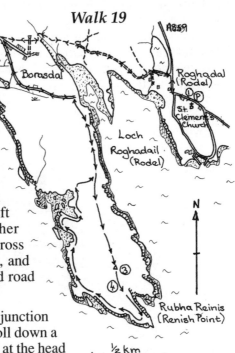

2 At the almost immediate Y-junction take the right branch to stroll down a very narrow road to its end at the head of Loch Rodel. Pass through a gate on the right and walk up onto the Renish headland (Rubha Reinis). Follow the fence, keeping to the right of it, as it climbs steadily upwards. On reaching a boundary fence ahead of you, bear right to a gate. Beyond, look for the cairn (50m) on the high ground ahead and cross over the pathless moorland, picking the easiest and the driest route to it. As you go notice the fine lazybeds that start on the drier ground and continue, sloping downwards, into a much wetter area.

3 Sit by the cairn and enjoy the fine view. Look east to see the Shiant Islands and, beyond, the mountains of mainland Scotland. Look

south-east to see the mountains on Skye. Due south, across the Sound of Harris, you can see the hills that form the spine of the Uists. To the south-west lie the islands of Killegray (Ceileagraigh) and Ensay (Easaigh), both uninhabited but with excellent grazing for sheep and cattle. Beyond these lies inhabited Berneray.

4 Then continue down the slopes to Renish Point (Rubha Reinis). Look for curious seals in the waters around the rocks and gannets flying fast over the sea. Eider ducks coo quietly from close inshore and oystercatchers and curlews call from a rocky fang projecting from the sea. Wind on round the rocky west shore, taking care as you edge the many inlets. At the fence bear right to go through the gate taken earlier and then retrace your outward route.

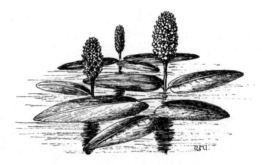

Amphibious Bistort

Practicals

Type of walk: A delightful, easy ramble. Maybe wet underfoot nearer the Point. Choose the best way over the heather moorland. Great views.

Distance:	5 ½ miles / 9km
Time:	2–3 hours. Add on time spent in the church.
Maps:	OS Explorer 455 / Landranger 18

20

Scalpay (Scalpaigh), off Harris

Park at the community centre, Kennavay (Ceann a' Bhaigh), on Scalpay, where there are toilets, grid ref. 215967. To reach this, leave Tarbert (Tairbeart) along the road leading east, signposted for Scalpay. Scalpay is now connected to the Harris mainland by a bridge, which cost £6 million to build and was opened in 1998. At the far end of the bridge, turn left, and then right at the junction. The community centre is beside the road in the middle of the village.

The village of **Kennavay** lies around the north and south harbours, both providing natural anchorage for boats. The pier was built in the 1960s.

A yellow pole against a rock face marks the well concealed cave that is believed to have provided a refuge for **Bonnie Prince Charlie** after the disastrous battle of Culloden. When this was discovered he hastily retreated to Uist from where Flora MacDonald rowed him across the Minch to Skye.

Scalpay lighthouse

& pier

71

Eilean Glas, constructed on its promontory in 1789, was one of the first lighthouses to be built in Scotland. The present tower was built between 1824 and 1826. It was designed by Robert Stevenson, the grandfather of Robert Louis Stevenson. The light is now automatic and its rays beam out over the Minch. Below the tower is a house which was occupied in 1789 by Alexander Reid, the first keeper, who lived in this lone outpost for 35 years.

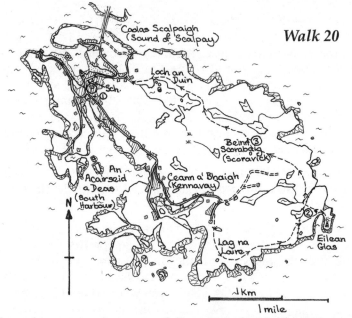

Walk 20

1 From the community centre, follow the quiet single track road as it leads you round beside South Harbour (An Acarsaid a Deas), and on through Kennavay. Just before the road end (2 miles from the bridge), take the way-marked footpath off to the left that leads across the hill to visit the famous cave at Lag na Laire. Keep to the left of the rocky hillock and descend nearly to the sea on the south side before turning left and following the way-marked route along above the shore. Look for puffins and guillemots fishing nearby and keep a watch for an elusive otter among the rocks or swimming through the seaweed. Once the lighthouse on Eilean Glas comes into view, make straight for it to reach its superbly built boundary wall. Turn left to follow the wall, going through the first gate you reach.

2 Wander the enclosed area, around the small harbour and then across the isthmus of Gneiss towards the red and white lighthouse with its large red foghorn. After enjoying this pleasing interlude, leave the enclosure by the main footpath which leads to another gate just to the north of a small lochan. Immediately you arrive outside the wall, turn right and follow the lighthouse wall nearly to its end, where way-markers direct you, left, uphill. The footpath leads past a group of small lochans then heads across a flat peaty area of Ben Scoravick (Beinn Scorabhaig). Climb up to the summit cairn which, at 343 ft / 104m, is the highest point on Scalpay. From here there is a fine view of Wester Ross, Skye and the Uists, as well as across to the Shiant Isles, North and South Harris and Lewis. Nearer at hand look for lazybeds and peat cuttings.

3 Follow the path downhill and where it bears down to the right and on over low hills to pass between two lochs. The second, Loch an Duin, is named after the crannog built towards the northern end which used to house a dun. The access causeway is now underwater due to the raising of the level of the loch. Follow the way-marked route as it swings round above the end of Loch an Duin before coming back down to the water. Keep close to the loch shore round the foot of the loch, where a good footbridge and stile give access to a track. This in turn brings you to a gate and then out to the road. Turn left and then left again at the T-junction to return to the village and your car.

Common Seal

Practicals

Type of walk: A delightful walk, full of interest and great views. The road walking is very quiet.

Distance:	7 miles / 11.4km
Time:	4–5 hours
Maps:	OS Explorer 455 / Landranger 14

21

Rhenigidale (Reinigeadal) and Todun, Harris

Park in large parking area at Urgha, just beyond the road bridge across the Laxadale Lochs, grid ref. 184004. To access this, leave Tarbert by the road to Kyles Scalpay (Caolas Scalpaigh).

Rhenigidale was settled in the 1820s by people who were evicted from the west side of Harris to leave their good pastures for sheep. Until 1989 the only access to the village was by boat or the route taken at the start of this walk. The new road is considered a blessing to the villagers, giving them access to shops and medical facilities. In the little settlement is a Gatliff Trust hostel, which provides basic accommodation.

South ridge of Todun

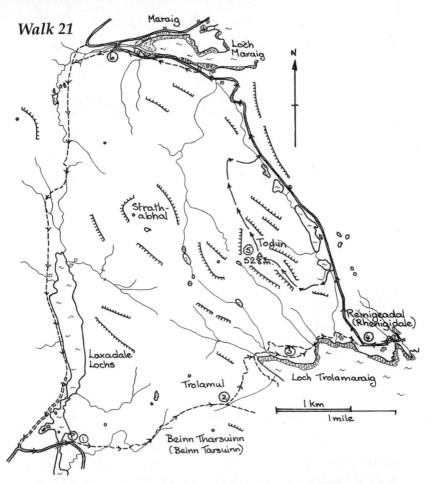

Walk 21

1 From the parking area take the footpath, signposted Rhenigidale. Follow the clear, reinforced, grassy path that climbs steadily upwards through heather moorland. Look for oak eggar moth caterpillars, making seemingly perilous crossings of the path. The Abhainn an t-Sratha bisects the path several times and you cross the lively burn on footbridges. As you climb, look left for your first sighting of Clisham. Watch out for gregarious golden plover and listen for their quiet piping. Continue on the long steady climb until you reach a cairn on the bealach (920 ft / 280m) between the tops of Beinn Tarsuinn (Tharsuinn) and Trollamul (Trolamul). From here there is a dramatic view of the Sound of Shiant, with the islands beyond and perhaps, on a clear day, the mainland of Scotland.

75

Below lies the sea loch Trollamarig (Trolamaraig).

2 Then begin your descent of the steep zig-zagging path, through deep peat, as it makes short tight bends down the side of Trollamul to the loch. To your left you can just glimpse the lovely waterfalls that plummet down the steep-sided Glen Trollamarig. Cross the bridge over the turbulent Abhainn Cheann an Locha as it races on its way to the loch. Here you may wish to pause to watch for otters and seals.

Northern Oak Eggar Moth

3 Carry on along the path to cross the Abhainn Kerram by bridge. The way then continues inland, zig-zagging more gently now, passing great whalebacks of Gneiss riven and scratched during glaciation. It carries on over Sron Mor. From here look back to see the cliff-path descended earlier. Walk on the clear way, cross more streams and go by several picturesque blackhouses. A pretty fall foams between two of the houses. Head on along the path past a small ravine, where rowan and willow thrive. Go through a gate and on to the junction with the 'new road'.

4 Turn right and walk into the settlement, its houses nestling around the tiny bay, where you will want to pause. Then return along the road, climbing steadily through the moonscape hills. To reach the summit of Todun, leave the road at the foot of the first loch you reach, circular Loch Beag, on your left. Cross the Abhainn Loteger on stepping stones. After wet weather, the burn can be in spate and difficult to cross, and the whole hillside becomes very wet and slippery. If so you may prefer to walk on along the road and give Todun a miss. To continue to the top of Todun, strike diagonally to your left across the gently sloping boggy moor. Continue round to reach the ridge at the earliest practicable point then make your way carefully up the ridge crest. This becomes quite narrow after a while and is rocky in places although there is a clear footpath along most of it. Pause to admire the spectacular views across southern Harris, to Clisham, the Park (Pairc) region of Lewis across Loch Seaforth, and the Shiant Isles and Skye. The summit (1658 ft / 528m) is marked by a trig point and has a surrounding wall as a shelter as the wind can be very strong.

5 After enjoying the superb view, descend by the north ridge, which is considerably less narrow than the south. Keep towards the right hand side (east) of the ridge as, when the slope shallows, you need to start bearing off to the right. Aim to rejoin the road well before it reaches the steep downhill section towards Loch Maraig but after it passes the last in the chain of lochans along the watershed. The flatter area between the ridge and the road can be boggy so make your way carefully across, keeping to drier ground where possible. At the road, turn left. As you descend Loch Seaforth, with its island, comes into view. Follow the road as it swings left beside Loch Maraig. Walk on to the head of the loch and as you approach the bridge over the Maraig River, look for a gate on the left of the road.

6 Pass through and walk the track, with the Maraig river to your right, signposted 'path to Tarbert'. Carry on to join the old pack road from Tarbert, where you walk sharply left (south). This leads you over wet moorland and climbs steadily along Braigh an Ruisg to a cairn. Beyond, the way descends steadily towards the Laxadale Lochs, with the track eventually running along the right bank, under the cliff face of Torsacleit. Carry on along the track until you reach the road from Tarbert. Turn left and walk down the slope, cross the bridge over the outflow from the Laxadale Lochs to rejoin your car.

Practicals

Type of walk: This is challenging and superb. Remote. Wonderful views. Paths and tracks wet in places and some road walking. Walking boots and good waterproofs essential. It is a long walk and weather on the Western Isles can change rapidly. Be prepared to turn back, or to forgo the climb to Todun. Or use two cars, leaving a second at the car park, grid ref. 194065. To reach this carry on along the 'new road' to where it joins the road to Tarbert. On the route to Rhenigidale there are several old paths turning off the main route. Ignore these; they were once used by the villagers but have now fallen into disrepair.

Distance:	12 ½ miles / 20km
Time:	7–8 hours
Maps:	OS Explorer 456 / Landranger 14

22

Island of Berneray (Bearnaraigh), by North Uist (Uibhist a Tuath)

Park at the community centre at Borve (Borgh), Berneray, grid ref. 910814. To reach this leave Lochmaddy (Loch nam Madadh) on North Uist by A865 and head north-west for five miles before turning right onto the B893. The causeway, built in 1999, sweeps dramatically across Berneray Sound, joining the island a short distance to the west of the slipway used by the ferry to Harris. Turn right at the main road and then left at Borve to reach the community centre at the end of the road.

Berneray is approximately 3 miles / 5km long and 1 ½ miles / 2.5km wide. The west side of the island is one long beach stretching for almost 3 miles / 5km, behind which is the machair. The island is in the parish of Harris and is now the only inhabited island in the Sound of Harris. It has two largish inland lochs, two sea lochs and two townships, Borve (Borgh) and Ruisgarry (Ruisgearraidh). The island contains no peat. In the early nineteenth century it was intensively cultivated and produced mainly potatoes and grain (in lazybeds) and kelp for soap and glass industries. But by the middle of the nineteenth century potato blight and cheaper substitutes for kelp had a huge effect

Standing Stone, Berneray

on the population and many families emigrated to Nova Scotia.

1 Return to the main road and cross to walk down to the little creek of Poll an Oir, sometimes used as a temporary harbour. Stride on along the main road to pass the jetty and harbour building, which was completed in 1989. Follow the road on around Bays Loch (Loch a' Bhaigh), with Borve Hill rising to

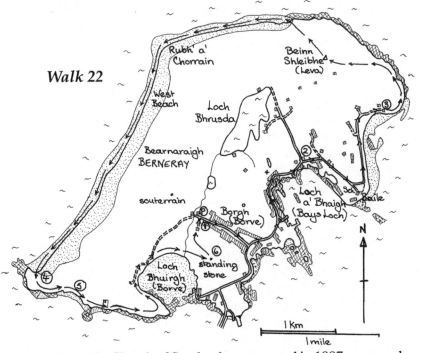

Walk 22

your left. At the Church of Scotland, constructed in 1887, you reach the boundary between the two townships.

2 At the Y-junction take the right branch. Just before the school, at Baile, look right to see several maintained blackhouses. All were built with double thickness walls. The group of blackhouses behind the school form the Gatliff Trust hostel, opened in 1977. Carry on along the narrow coast road. Look left to see, on a rocky hillock, the gaunt ruins of a church. This was built by the nineteenth century engineer Thomas Telford and had two entrance doors, one for the people of Berneray and the other for the folk from the nearby island of Pabbay (Pabaigh). The people rowed over the Pabbay Sound, called by a great bell that sounded for miles.

3 At the road end go through a gate and follow the way-markers along the shore. This is a favoured spot of turnstones. Once beyond the cross fence, carry on as directed by the way-marks to the summit of Ben Leva (Beinn Shleibhe), 305 ft / 93m, from where there is a superb view over to Pabbay, Boreray (Boraraigh) and maybe St Kilda. From the summit take the path heading straight down to the end of the sandy beach. Continue along the lovely sands to Rubh' a' Chorrain, where the beach (West Beach) curves south-west. To your left sand dunes, some 6–9m high, tower upwards, held firmly by marram grass. Stroll the glorious shell-sand, which has a scattering of many species of seaweed, where you might see ringed plover hurrying through the weed after sand flies. Carry on to the end of the sands (2 ¼ miles from Rubh' a' Chorrain).

Corn Marigold

4 Just above the shore here stones were set into the ground to support seaweed for drying and burning, when the industry was thriving. This western tip of Berneray is named Braighe na Ceilp, meaning Breastwork of the Kelp. Here wind on round the south shore of the island, overlooking the Berneray Sound, to come to a tall man-made cairn, which is surrounded by a small wall and odd stones. The cairn was erected in 1991 to commemorate Angus MacAskill, who lived almost 145 years ago. Angus, a giant 7ft 9 inches in height, was born in a croft on the site of the cairn. He left Berneray when he was six, emigrating with his family to Nova Scotia. He was reputed to be the strongest man in the world. The *Guinness Book of Records* states that Angus was a non-pathological, or true, giant. The cairn has been built 7ft 9 inches high.

5 Continue along the edge of the sound, heading towards a walled burial cairn. Most of the cemeteries in the Western Isles are built on a slope and facing the sea. The majority are found on the west coast; on the east there is not enough soil for burial. Walk on along the low headland until the sea loch, Loch Borve (Loch Bhuirgh) comes into view. This wide stretch of water has pleasing sandy margins and at low tide the water recedes completely, exposing an entire sandy bed. As you near the loch, join a grassy track that runs beside it. Cross a stone bridge over a stream and then continue until you can follow way-markers, leading you right, up the slopes of Beinn a' Claidh to a fine standing stone. It is 8ft in height and dates back to around 2,000 BC. Then walk a little way south for about 120m to look for the difficult-to-find Stone of the King. It has the imprint of a human foot and may have been used in the inauguration of a king.

6 Return down to the track and continue to the community centre at Borve, where you might see a short-eared owl, hunting beside the road, often perching on fence posts. Here you might wish to locate the Chairstone. To do this, walk in front of the building to climb a stile. Strike ahead, bearing slightly left, towards a number of boulders that rise above the pasture. Look for two that are shaped like seats. These are believed to have been in use during Viking times and were used during the settling of disputes, the largest for the judge and the one opposite for the accused. Then return to the community centre where you may be able to obtain refreshments.

Corncrake

Practicals

Type of walk: A long, fairly level glorious ramble, one that needs a good day to really appreciate the glorious sands, the machair and the views. If you do not have time for the complete walk the route could be broken down into several short, linear ones.

Distance: 11 miles / 18km
Time: 6–7 hours
Maps: OS Explorer 454 / Landranger 18

23

Grenitote (Greinetobht) Headland, North Uist (Uibhist a Tuath)

Park in the good parking area constructed above the beach, grid ref. 819756. To reach this, leave the A865 at Grenitote and drive through the village to the end of the sealed road.

In July 1998 the **townships of Sollas (Solas) and Grenitote** celebrated 100 years of crofting with ceilidhs, walks, talks and cockle picking at Udal. Descendants of former islanders came from as far away as the United States, Canada, Australia, and New Zealand to swell the large numbers of tourists and the small local population. Two plaques commemorate the celebrations.

This is **a wonderful walk for bird-watching**. Look for bar-tailed godwits, among other waders on the Grenitote Strand. Take care as you cross the machair not to disturb nesting dunlin, ringed plover and snipe. Among the cereal and potato crops nest Arctic terns and a few little terns. Watch for Arctic skuas harrying the terns to drop their sand eel meal they have caught for their young. Look out to sea for gannets fishing.

N. Uist hills from Rubha Velish, Grenitote

1 Leave the parking area by the vehicle track leading down to the beach and cross the shallow stream on stepping stones. Follow the track as it continues along the top of the beach below the grassy turf, with a fence to your left.

2 After nearly 1km a distinct track leads off to the left between two fenced areas of cultivated machair. At the end of the enclosures, bear right along the track to pass between the dunes and the cultivated machair.

3 Follow the track round to the left to make your way over the narrow neck of the dunes to reach Velish Point (Rubha Bheilis). From here you get wonderful views back down West Beach (Traigh an Iar) to the hills of North Uist as well as out to the Hasgeir Islands and St Kilda. Return over the dunes to the track. Continue north along the coast, again avoiding the cultivated areas. Inland on a knoll is an excavated site, possibly in use from Bronze Age times until late in the seventeenth century when a sandstorm engulfed the village. Do not disturb the site.

Walk 23

Artic Skua chasing Tern

83

4 Head on along the coast, past Huilish Point and then Traigh Udal. Continue to the high dune system ahead, and take the good path up Aird a' Mhorain to the trig point (40m) at the north end of the beach.

5 Go on round the headland, keeping to the east side of the peninsula to go by the cemetery of the MacLeans of Boreray, where nearby rocks have Bronze Age cup markings. Stroll on, heading south, along the rough track or walk the sands to cross the sandspit, Corran Aird a' Mhorain.

6 Press on along your outward route to return to Grenitote. If the tide is too high on your return, turn right through a gate just before the stepping stones crossed at the outset. Go through several more gates, pass a ruined building and then on along a walled field. Stroll a grassy trod left, to another gate leading to the minor road to Sollas. From here stride left along the main road to Grenitote.

Frog Orchid

Practicals

Type of walk: This glorious walk takes you along easy paths, tracks and sandy shores around a long finger of land that juts northwards from North Uist into a turquoise sea.

Distance: 8 ½ miles / 13.7km. The diversion because of very high tides adds 1 ¼ miles / 2km to the walk.
Time: 3–4 hours
Maps: OS Explorer 454 / Landranger 18

24

Beinn Scolpaig, North Uist

Park on the turf beyond a large unmarked passing area, grid ref. 752750. Ahead lies Loch Olavat (Olabhat). To reach this, take the A865 north west from Lochmaddy to skirt the coast and turn off at the narrow road leading to Loch Olavat.

Scolpaig tower, the Western Isles' only folly, is situated on an old prehistoric site, a dun, on a green islet in the west bay of Loch Scolpaig. It was commissioned by Dr Alex MacLeod between 1830 and 1840, some say to provide work for the people. Alas the stones of the dun were used to build the tower. Fulmars make full use of ledges in the walls to nest and mute swans, little grebes, mallard duck and tufted duck nest in the large nearby reedbed.

Scolpaig Tower

Scolpaig Tower

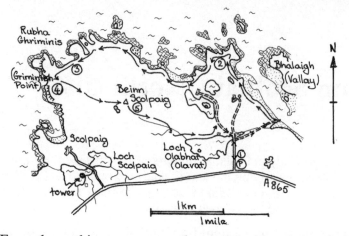

1 From the parking area, cross the cattle grid and, just before the causeway over the north end of Loch Olavat, follow a narrow road that swings right. Continue until you reach the pier overlooking Valley Sound (Caolas Bhalaigh), where several colourful fishing boats are moored. Beyond the sound lies the island of Valley, separated from the mainland, at low tide, by Valley Strand, a wide expanse of silver sand. Walk left (north west), along the edge of the Sound, with a fence to your left and the gently lapping water and the sandy shore

Rabbit

to your right. Pass through a gate and continue along a grassy footpath to pass a large circular house. Go through a gap in the fence and then through another gate to lead you out onto the sandy turf. Stroll on along the way, which is alive with rabbits and starlings—perhaps the most common bird to be seen in the Western Isles.

2 Continue ahead past several glorious bays white with shell sand. At the fence, either walk right and clamber over easily-negotiated rocks or walk left to a gate in the fence. The next bay is full of jagged rocks, thrusting into the sea. Great cobalt-blue rollers come roaring in and break on the rocks with huge fountains of white foam. Keep to the right of the fence running below Beinn Scolpaig and follow it to the end, where again you need to scramble over

86

Dabchicks (Little Grebes)

rocks. Carry on ahead around Griminish Point (Rubha Ghriminis). Proceed with care to a large hole in the green turf. Peer over to see large bubbles of foam covering the floor of a deep cavern created when the roof collapsed. Walk round the gaping hole and then move over to the edge of the cliffs, again with care, to see the foam of the waves being forced through an arch in the cliff, connecting the cavern.

3 Head on along the cliffs until you can see the lovely sands of Scolpaig, with Scolpaig farm beyond. At this point you can see Scolpaig Tower.

4 Then strike left, up a path, ascending the slopes of Beinn Scolpaig, crossing two small hillocks and keeping to the left of Loch Sniogrivat before attaining the trig point at 298 ft / 91m. Pause here to enjoy the extensive view. Look across the Vallay Sands to see the Harris Hills. Beyond Hasgeir Island, you can just discern St Kilda.

5 From the trig point you can also see your car parked beyond Loch Olavat. Drop down the slope, following a shallow valley beside the loch outflow, aiming for a gate in the fence behind a ruined hut. Once through continue ahead, bearing slightly left to avoid a wettish area. On reaching the boundary wall, walk left to a gate in a fence. Stride ahead along a short stony track and then turn right along the causeway over the loch. Press ahead to where you have parked.

Practicals

Type of walk: An easy ramble round the cliffs, followed by a short ascent to a fine viewpoint. At the right time of the year listen for corncrakes.

Distance:	5 miles / 8km
Time:	2–3 hours
Maps:	OS Explorer 454 / Landranger 18

25

Balranald RSPB Nature Reserve, North Uist

Park in the car park at the reserve, grid ref. 705706. To access this, take the A865 from Lochmaddy along the west coast of the island and turn right for Hougharry. At the Y-junction take the left branch and continue to the reserve.

Balranald (Baile Raghnaill) RSPB Nature Reserve was established in 1966 in agreement with three landowners, together with the approval of the crofting townships of Tigharry (Tigh a' Ghearraidh), Hougharry (Hogha Gearraidh), Goular and Balranald. The reserve is composed of a rich mosaic of habitats; rocky headlands, sandy bays, dunes, machair, grassland, marshes and lochs. It is composed entirely of crofting land and walkers are asked to show consideration for the people who work there, and their stock, crops and fencing. For the best time to see and hear the wildlife, visit in spring and summer. But Balranald has something of interest for visitors at any time of the year, given the beauty and the wildness of the place. Signposting is kept to a minimum to preserve the appearance of the landscape.

Traigh nam Faoghailean, Balranald

Walk 25

1 Leave the car park and follow the track, west, along behind the beach. Continue on the main track as it swings right, ignoring a few side branches, to cross an area of cultivated machair. At the end of the track, pass through a gate, ensuring you close it firmly behind you, as the area is used to graze cattle. Pass the end of Loch a' Roe, off to your right, and stay with the footpath as it skirts the beach. As you go, look inland where you might spot a hen harrier hunting across the reserve.

2 Look out to sea towards the Monach Isles, a National Nature Reserve, where thousands of grey seals come to breed. Carry on round above the beach to pass between the shore and a second lochan. On a clear day you should see, to the west, Hasgeir Islands and St Kilda. Follow the footpath as it continues to skirt above the shore.

3 As you approach Eilean Trostain notice the lines of rounded raised turf, 'lazy beds'. The humpy ridges were used to grow potatoes, fertilised by seaweed to improve the soil depth and drainage. The beds were cultivated by the people of Hougharry and close by was the original site of their village. Notice the prominent rock 'the big rock of the farthing' where the villagers once came to pay their rents.

4 Head down across the grazed pasture to pass through another fastened gate. Continue over the sand dunes and past cultivated machair. Go down onto the lovely shell sand bay, Traigh nam Faoghailean, where you will

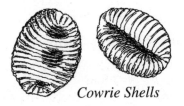

Cowrie Shells

89

want to dawdle. Look for the little pink and white cowry shells that litter the strand line.

5 If the tide is low, continue to the end of the beach to pass below the houses, scrambling carefully over the rock slabs. Just before you reach another sandy beach, cut up to the right to pass a building and gain access to the road. Turn left and then right to follow a narrow road behind Hougharry, then cross the next road. Take the track behind the beach until you can return to the visitor centre.

6 If the tide is too high, leave the beach before you reach the village, by climbing over the grassy bank and returning along the track to the visitor centre. Listen out for corncrakes in the long vegetation here.

Corn Bunting

Practicals

Type of walk: This delightful easy walk is full of interest.

Distance: 4 ½ miles / 7.4km
Time: 3 hours
Maps: OS Explorer 454 / Landranger 18

26

Uneval (Uineabhal), North Uist

Park in a large lay-by on the north side of the A867, grid ref. 812642. To reach this leave Lochmaddy by the A867 and once past the B894 turn-off for Loch Eport (Euphort), park in an old quarry on the right.

Souterrains are stone-walled underground passageways. They were usually attached to a stone or timber roundhouse. Some had two entrances one to the house and the other to the outside. As they maintained a constant low temperature they may have been used for storage, such as grain or meat, the food put in one end and removed from the house end as and when needed. It has been suggested they may have been refuges or even shrines.

Chambered Cairn, Uineabhal (Uneval)

1 Walk back a few yards and turn left, onto a metalled track opposite the B894. Continue past an old quarry (where you might find alternative parking) and stride on. Where the track divides, take the right fork, with a fenced area on the right, to walk on along a short peaty track out onto heather moorland. Ahead stands the hill Uneval (460 ft / 140m).

2 Where the fence swings away to the right, bear diagonally left, past peat banks to walk over the Druim Langara, the plateau towards the west slope of Uneval. Look for great skuas here. Gradually descend from the plateau, traversing the boggy moorland, keeping to the right of two small lochans and right also of the much larger Loch Huna, which lies west of the two smaller lochans. Carry on ahead to pass between Loch Huna still to your left and another lochan to your right. To make sure you are heading in the right direction, look for the very green patch on the right slope (east) of Uneval. The lochan on your right receives water from Loch Huna and this outlet stream needs to be crossed at the narrowest point. The best place is just before it joins the small lochan, where yellow water lilies grow.

Walk 26

3 Once across, return along the side of the stream. Then continue around Loch Huna, following deer tracks for the easiest way. Here look for otter spraints. Once beyond its northern end, carry on to climb the slope to the green patch to see the remains of the souterrain. From this green grassy area, encircled by peaty moorland, you can see the large chambered cairn below Ben Langass, visited on Walk 27. Look down on Loch Huna for a good view of its crannog.

4 Then contour west round Uneval until you reach the large standing stone. (If you decide to climb to the summit before descending to the standing stone, be prepared for a splendid view but also for a very wet plateau, with high peat hags to be negotiated.) Near the stone are the remains of a chambered cairn and an iron-age-house. What strategic sites these prehistoric people chose; they could see for many miles.

5 From the standing stone, look down to see the gate through the fence, half a mile across the moor. To reach this drop down the slope and walk, with care, the wet area between Loch na Buail' Iochdraich and the south west side of Loch Huna. Beyond the gate walk diagonally left to a gate close to Loch Huna, where white and yellow water lilies grow together. Once through this second gate, climb Druim Langara, still heading slightly left. Continue until the fenced area of improved land comes into view. Beside it is the peaty track which soon joins the road.

Great Skua

Practicals

Type of walk: A challenging but great walk over often wet moorland to see more prehistoric sites. Choose a good day.

Distance: 6 miles / 9.8km
Time: 3–4 hours
Maps: OS Explorer 454 / Landranger 18

27

Ben Langass (Beinn Langais) North Uist

Park in the little quarry on the south side of the A867, grid ref. 834658. To reach this leave Lochmaddy by the A867 and park in the quarry just before the signposted turning to the Langass Lodge Hotel.

The **oval-shaped stone circle** is known as Finn's People (Pobull Fhinn). There are around 48 stones, with only half of them still standing. The circle stands on the south side of Ben Langass, on a platform cut into the uphill side and built up on the downhill side. It was probably constructed between 3,000 BC and 1500 BC. Stand in the circle and enjoy the grand view of the lochs and islands of North Uist and of the small range of hills, from North Lee (Li a Tuath) to Eaval (Eabhal).

Barpa Langass is a neolithic chambered cairn, possibly used first in the second or third millennium BC and later in the early Bronze Age and concealed by an enormous cairn of stone. It seems to have been used as a collective burial site for the local inhabitants

Chambered Cairn, Barpa Langass

of the area and possibly for rituals. It is situated on the north-west shoulder of Ben Langass. Beyond a small entrance and two stone lintels, is the burial chamber. It has a charming skirt of heather and various ferns.

1 Walk west along the A-road for a short distance to take the signposted left turn for the hotel. Just before the end of the track (¾ mile / 1.4km), take the timber boardwalk leading left up the slope through heather and bracken to reach the stone circle, where you will want to pause. Below lies Loch Langass, a long stretch of sparkling water part of a huge tidal sea loch that joins the sea through Loch Eport (Loch Euphort).

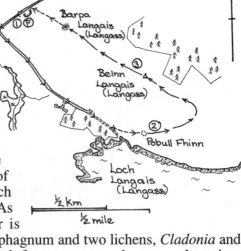

Loch a' Bharpa

Walk 27

N

Barpa Langais (Langass)

Belnn Langais (Langass)

Pobull Fhinn

Loch Langais (Langass)

½ Km
½ mile

2 Then follow the way-marker posts to the summit of Ben Langass (298 ft / 91m) from where you can see a necklace of lochs. Below there is much evidence of peat cutting. As you ascend the heather is replaced by deer grass, sphagnum and two lichens, *Cladonia* and reindeer moss. On its north face you come close to a plantation, planted in 1969 by the Forestry Commission (FC) Research Branch. Eventually the trees began to make good growth and, with the shelter provided, the FC has been able to introduce rowan, birch, alder, aspen and willow. You may wish to make a detour into the plantation before continuing on.

White Waterlily

3 From the little summit drop down the slope towards a great mound of stones, the chambered cairn. From here follow the way-marked route back to where you have parked. As you go, look out for hen harrier, buzzard, kestrel, peregrine, short eared owl and maybe a golden eagle.

Short-eared Owl

Practicals

Type of walk: This short moorland walk is full of interest.

Distance:	3 ½ miles / 5.8km
Time:	2–3 hours
Maps:	OS Explorer 454 / Landranger 18

28

Eaval (Eabhal), North Uist

Park at the end of the road where there is a good parking area, grid ref. 891632. To access this, leave Lochmaddy by the A867 and after seven miles take the B894, signposted Locheport (Loch Euphort) and Sidinish (Saighdinis). The B-road runs along a small ridge above the sea loch, Loch Eport, which lies to the left.

Choose a day when the tide is out so that the **stepping stones** between Loch Obisary (Loch Obasaraigh) and Loch Eport present no problems both on the way to Eaval and on the return. North Uist Estates would be grateful if you do not use this route beyond

Eaval & Loch Obisary

Burrival (Burabhal) (or other routes to Eaval) when deer are calving in late June to early July or at stalking times (Sundays excepted), September to October.

Looking north, from the top of **Eaval**, you can see the hills of North Harris and the Lewis coast beyond. Nearer you can see Chaipaval, Hushinish and Berneray. And then to the west lie the magnificent sands of North Uist and the islands of Baleshare (Baile Sear) and Kirkibost (Chircebost). Out to sea beyond the Monach Islands you can discern St Kilda and Boreray. South and below, lies Benbecula, with more water than land, the latter linked with seemingly tiny strings, the causeways. It looks as if the next gale could blow the land out to sea. Beyond lie the hills of South Uist. To the east the Kintail hills are visible. Nearer, on Skye, you can see the Tables of MacLeod, Loch Dunvegan, Vaternish Point, Trotternish, Loch Bracadale, and the Kiskavaig cliffs and, over all, the peaks of the Cuillin. And as you swing round to face Harris once more, the Shiants come into view.

Walk 28

1 Go through the small gate beyond the parking space and head on, passing to the right of a crofthouse. Follow the track as it curves right and then left to pass through another gate. Follow the fence posts over the moor to pass a small bay with a sturdy wall of stones, creating a little harbour. Climb the heathery path and continue across a wet area to walk past another small bay, where you might spot a heron, patiently waiting for its prey. The track leads to a bank of stones across the outflow stream from the freshwater Loch Obisary (Obasaraigh). The tide comes in on the left of the stones and its water flows in to Loch Obisary. Look for patches of seaweed on the freshwater side.

2 Cross the stepping stones and walk out onto the moor, taking a path through the softly-scented heather. Follow it as it swings right and keeps above a very wet area full of large pools. Ahead lies Burrival (460 ft / 140m), a solid, round-topped hill where ravens congregate. Press on along an often indistinct way, aiming for the gate in the fence ahead, slightly to the right of centre of Burrival.

Rock Doves

3 Once beyond the gate continue on towards the formidable-looking Eaval, which now lies to your right across Loch Obisary. To reach it, turn right and begin the delightful walk, skirting Burrival, using clear tracks made by deer, sheep and humans along the heathery slopes of Loch Obisary's many small bays. The loch, a photographer's paradise, has many small islands, all lush with vegetation that is out of reach of the voracious sheep. Cross the fence at the head of the loch and continue.

4 When you reach the narrow but deep outflow stream from Loch Surtavat hurrying to reach Loch Obisary, walk upstream to find an easy place to cross. Then begin the gradual ascent of the northeast slopes of Eaval. These are a glorious mix of long outcrops of Gneiss, giving good grip for walking boots, and long hollows of grass and heather sloping upwards between the rock. Look for clumps of fir clubmoss and sprigs of juniper thriving. As you climb, more and more familiar islands, hills, lochs and peaks come into view. And then suddenly you are at the summit, where stands a triangulation point set in a cairn enclosed within a stone shelter. The view is stunning. All round the hill lie many lochs, fitting together as neatly as a jig-saw.

5 Leave the summit by the route taken to ascend, aiming for the sandy shores of small bays at the head of Loch Obisary. Return from here by the same route.

Fir Clubmoss

Practicals

Type of walk: This is a glorious challenge but expect some wet ground to cross. Suitable for experienced hill walkers. Check tide tables. Be prepared to turn back if the outflow stream from Loch Surtavat is in spate.

Distance: 9–10 miles / 14.5–16km
Time: 5–6 hours
Maps: OS Explorer 454 / Landranger 18 and 22

29

Island of Flodda (Flodaigh), Benbecula (Beinn na Faoghla)

Park in the open area beside the A865, grid ref. 820557. To reach this, and if travelling from the north, cross the causeway that unites North Uist with Benbecula. Then look for the second road junction on the left and park near the corner.

The Western Isles have many magnificently constructed **causeways**. Benbecula was linked to South Uist in 1942 and to North Uist in 1963. In 1990 Vatersay was linked to Barra by a causeway at a cost of £3 million. Scalpay was connected to the Harris mainland in 1998 at a cost of £6 million. The island of Berneray was linked to North Uist in 1999. Work on the causeway between Eriskay and South Uist was started in May 2000 and was in use from July 12, 2001. It was officially opened on September 11, 2002. The total cost was £9.8 million; this included ferry terminals for the vehicular ferry between Eriskay and Barra. Flodda is linked to

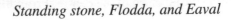

Standing stone, Flodda, and Eaval

A865
Gramasdail

N

standing
stone

Caolas
Fhlodaigh
(Sound of Flodda)

Flodaigh
(Flodda)

1 Km
1 mile

Benbecula by a causeway and there are several more smaller causeways throughout the Isles, all making life easier for people going about their daily lives, working and socialising. How their ancestors would have appreciated them.

1 Walk the narrow lane, where willow and irises grow. Pass a lochan and stride on along a small causeway across the end of a second lochan, where white water lilies flower. To the left is a good view of Eaval (walk 28). Just before a stone-built causeway over a sea

Common Seals

inlet, there is a blackhouse on the left of the road and two gates on the right. Pass through one of the gates and climb the hill on an indistinct path. Go through a gate in the fence to reach the standing stone, which appears to be all that is left of a stone circle, possibly with a burial cairn in the centre. From this small eminence there is a pleasing view of the hills and the many areas of water, both fresh and salt. Away to the east, the mountains of Skye stand out with startling clarity in the wonderfully clear light.

2 Return to the road and carry on over the causeway and then follow the road as it moves out into open moorland. Go on past another inland loch and stroll on to a causeway over the Sound of Flodda (Caolas Fhlodaigh) and continue to the turning area at the end of the road. Go through the gate onto the right-hand track and then through a second gate after this. Follow the track down and round the corner, and at a signpost to 'Seals' turn right along a good path and through a gate. By another sign the path swings left beside a fence; follow this down and round to meet a sea inlet. Here seals pup on the skerries. There are many common seals and their pups, and you may also see mergansers with ducklings at the right time of year, and if you are lucky, a peregrine falcon. There are splendid views of the Skye Cuillin, the Rum Cuillin and Hecla.

3 Continue on along the path round the coast. Where the fence divides, cross it at a broken place and follow a small footpath beside the branch, which heads inland. This brings you through a second gap in another fence to rejoin your outward route by the second sign. Retrace your steps up the path and track to return to the road.

Yellow Iris

Practicals

Type of walk: All minor road walking. Good track and paths. A pleasing evening walk.

Distance: 4 ½ miles / 7.2km
Time: 2–3 hours
Maps: OS Explorer 453 / Landranger 22

30

Rueval (Ruabhal) and Rossinish (Roisinis), Benbecula

Park in the parking area at the end of the road, by the landfill site, grid ref. 810535. To reach this, drive south along the A865 over the causeway that connects North Uist with Benbecula. After 2 ½ miles / 4km, turn left and continue for half a mile to park on the left.

Under one of the overhangs on the south-east face of Rueval, and well hidden by heather, Bonnie Prince Charlie lay hidden for two days. At the battle of Culloden Moor, April 16 1746, his army had been beaten. Charles and his friends managed to escape (with a price of £30,000 on his head). By June 20 the Prince and his companions were hiding on Rueval, Benbecula, waiting for news of a boat in which to get away from the Western Isles. On June 26, after hearing that Flora MacDonald had obtained a boat, they set off to walk to **Rossinish** to join her. It is believed that they spent

North Uist from Rueval

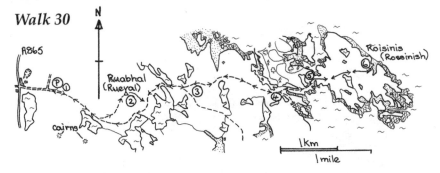

two days here. Then they crossed to Skye and stayed at Monkstadt. After more journeying and hiding Charles, on Sept. 20, boarded a French ship, never to return to Scotland again.

1 Take the signed track across the cattle grid and follow it to Loch Ba Una. About two-thirds of the way along the side of the loch there is a grassy track, on the left, heading up Rueval (409 ft / 124m), the latter heather-covered and with several craggy overhanging outcrops below the top. Follow the track as it winds uphill and turns into a good path that skirts a fenced enclosure. Follow the path right up onto the summit as it leads across rocky ridges to the trig point and two cairns. There are fine views all round from the summit of Rum, Skye, Hecla, and up to the Hasgeir Islands and Harris.

2 Below you can see the continuing track to Rossinish as it winds between the lochans. Head down the hill to join this at its nearest point, bearing round right to avoid the steepest ground. There is no clear footpath but the ground is fairly easy. Or if you prefer, descend by your upward route and walk on along the

Stonechat

track to pass Loch Hermidale (Loch Theirmeadail) and then Loch na Deighe fo Dheas, both on the right. From here there are good views of Eaval (walk 28). Cross a small turf causeway between

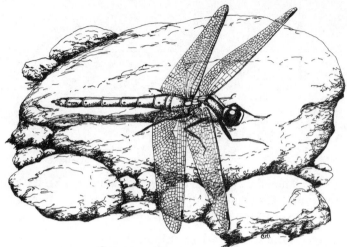

Common Darter

Loch na Deighe fo Thuath and the north end of Loch na Deighe fo Dheas and go on along the gated track. Where the track divides, take the left fork.

3 Ahead are more good views of Skye. Pass the head of Loch an Tairbh and look for the shieling away to the left on a hillock beyond a gate. To the right is a sheep fank, an enclosure where sheep are gathered. As you continue, look right to see the tops of Hecla and Beinn Mhor in South Uist. To the left lies Flodda (walk 29), and beyond its headland you might spot the many seals on the small islands in the Sound of Flodda. Carry on along the track, past an inlet from the Sound. Very soon the way is almost obscured by heather, with clumps of white among the pink. To the right across a loch stands a ruined crofthouse.

4 Stride the track as it crosses another grassy causeway, with salt water to the right and fresh to the left. The track then leads through more heather gardens with a loch to your left where honeysuckle hangs over the water. The route then continues as a narrow path on a small cliff above the loch. To the right, on an inlet of the sea, look for rowan and aspen, clinging to a low cliff face.

5 Then you come to a gate and here you must make a decision. Perhaps this is as far as you wish to walk, and you might prefer to sit by one of the inlets of the sea, enjoying the view. If however,

you want to reach Rossinish, a deserted crofthouse, you need to be able to map read because there are no paths. There is a small path to a tiny beach but from then on it is best to follow animal tracks in an easterly direction across the rather wet moorland to the side of the largest of three inland lochs. Walk round the northern end of it and then continue ahead to the house.

6 When you arrive be prepared for a surprise. The peaty moorland suddenly becomes sandy and the house is dwarfed by towering sand dunes. In front of the ruin is a grassy sward and below a delightful sandy creek. Bonnie Prince Charlie left here by boat, dressed as a serving maid, for Skye. After a pause here and perhaps a ponder on his thoughts as he waited for Flora, you need to return by the same route, enjoying all the views you missed on your outward trek.

Otter

Practicals

Type of walk: The track provides easy walking but can be wet in places. The views have a charm of their own. Wet moorland to be crossed from the gate to Rossinish.

Distance:	9 miles / 14.5km
Time:	5–6 hours
Maps:	OS Explorer 453 / Landranger 22

31

Druidibeg (Druidibeag) and Howmore (Tobha Mor), South Uist (Uibhist a Deas)

Park at the Information Point by Loch Druidibeg, grid ref. 789382. To access this leave the A865, left, on the B890 just before Hopewell Cottage, if travelling south from Benbecula.

There is so much to see at **Howmore**, a very picturesque village. In an ancient walled burial ground there are many gravestones. This was the graveyard of the ClanRanald chiefs. Look for the scant ruins of three small chapels, one of which was the burial chapel for the ClanRanald chiefs, and two churches. All the masonry is heavily encrusted with usnea and an orange lichen. In its day this is believed to have been a college and a monastery, a great centre of learning. It was destroyed during the Reformation. It was from this site that the ClanRanald Armorial Stone was stolen in 1990. It has since been recovered and is housed in Kildonan Museum. Close by is the youth hostel, a thatched blackhouse run by the Gatliff

Loch Druidibeg with Hecla & Beinn Corradail

Trust. They have restored more cottages. Leave time to visit the austere church, which has a central communion pew, one of only two in Scotland. Here you might hear corncrakes.

At the end of your walk you may wish to continue along the Loch Skipport (Loch Sgioport) road for three quarters of a mile to visit the plantation, part of the **Loch Druidibeg National Nature Reserve**. It was originally planted by the owners of South Uist Estates. In 1958 it was purchased by the reserve, who erected a deer fence around the area. In 1968 many native trees were planted. It now has a variety of trees including birch, hazel, alder, Norway maple, Scots pine and three monkey puzzle trees. It is a good place to watch woodland birds.

Walk 31

1 Stroll back down the B-road beside Loch Druidibeg, which is famed for its breeding greylag geese, to the junction with the A865. Cross the road and walk the track. Carry on to pass Grogarry (Groigearraidh) Lodge and continue on to the machair, in summer a riot of colourful flowers. As you pass Loch Grogarry (Groigearraidh), turn left and walk on to a stile into a pasture.

2 Cross the footbridge over a wide dyke and walk on south, with the loch to your left and the dunes away to your right. When you reach a reinforced track, going off left, ignore this and carry on, with Loch Stilligarry (Stadhlaigearraidh) now to your left, to reach Drimsdale House at the end of the road from Drimsdale (Dreumasdal).

Greylag Geese

3 Here you may like to turn inland (¼ mile / 0.5km) to see, on your right, the romantic ruined castle, Caisteal Bheagram, on its island on Loch an Eilean (Loch an Eilein). Return to the machair and carry on along the track, where you might disturb dozens of greylag geese. Where the track divides, take the left branch to come to the church and the ruined college and monastery at Howmore, where you will want to dawdle and enjoy the wonderfully peaceful atmosphere.

4 Return along the track. Ignore the turn to Drimsdale and go on with Loch Stilligarry now away to your right, to take the next turn inland to return to the A865.

5 Cross to take the track ahead (east of the A-road) towards some houses. Bear right past a way-marked post just before the last house and take the gate onto open land. Head across towards the loch before swinging left to pass an old ruin. There are stone-built causeways across the wettest areas. On the third of these, pass through a gate to cross a stone bridge over the burn connecting the two lochs and follow the clear way-marked path round to the right.

Tufted Ducks

6 Go through another gate and then a third. The path winds through old peat cuttings taking a careful tortuous route which avoids the wettest areas. At the end of the peat cuttings follow a fence to the left to come to two parallel gates, then head up the track to return to the parking place. As the way-marked route leads you across the reserve notice the islands in the Loch, which support rowan, willow and juniper, out of reach of voracious sheep and deer.

Bog Pimpernel

Practicals

Type of walk: A good walk over a variety of different habitats, with much to see as you go.

Distance:	8 miles / 13km plus the 1 ½ miles / 2.5km if you walk to and from the plantation.
Time:	5 hours
Maps:	OS Explorer 453 / Landranger 22

32

Rubha Ardvule (Rubha Aird a'Mhuile), South Uist

Park on either side of a track, on the machair, beyond the fencing, grid ref. 729299. To reach this take a turn off the A865, signposted for Bornish (Bornais). After less than a mile the road swings right to Ormiclate (Ormacleit) Castle, which you ignore. Continue ahead past the priest's house on the left and then Bornish House on the right. Pass the Catholic church and continue on to park.

St Mary's church, near where you have parked, has a very interesting interior. Go inside to see the unrendered walls of Gneiss and the plain oak pews. All this simplicity acts as a foil to the dramatically-draped altar and colourful robes of the Virgin Mary.

Rubha Ardvule (Rubha Aird a'Mhuile) is the most westerly point to South Uist. A rough road/track winds out to the point, passing Dun Vulan, an Iron Age broch, now a ruin. The little headland is a wonderful place in any weather and ideal for a picnic on a sunny day. It is also an anchorage for local fishing boats.

South Uist hills from Rubha Ardvule

Ormiclate Castle (Caisteal Ormacleit), built in 1701 by French masons and overseen by a French architect, took 7 years to construct. It was built for the French wife of Allan, the ClanRanald chief and occupied for 7 years. It accidentally burned down in 1715, on the eve of the battle of Sherriff Muir, where the chief was fatally wounded. Although now a lichen-clad roofless ruin it is easy to imagine how grand it was in its day.

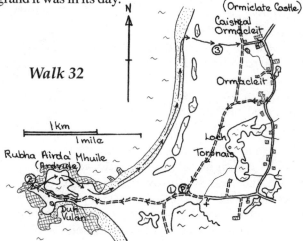

Walk 32

1 Walk ahead on the reinforced track through pasture land, where cattle graze. Beyond this, stroll on beside acres of oats, where you should keep a watchful eye for a corncrake. These birds spend much time in iris beds and rear their young in long grass or in a field of oats. Stride on along the rough 'road' where it moves out onto the headland. Here you might spot brightly painted boats sheltering in the lee of a curving bay. Half way along the track, look for a circular pile of stones, all that remains of Dun Vulan. To your right lies Loch Ardvule, a lovely stretch of water. The outlet of the loch, at the tip of the little headland, is blocked by a plug of boulders thrown up by the sea.

Large red Damselfly

2 Where the track ends, cross the narrow strip of land and the spit of boulders and continue round the headland. Look here for the stalks of kelp drying in beehive-shaped piles that stand on a bed of boulders. The kelp, washed up in vast quantities, is sold for

113

pharmaceutical purposes. You will want to pause here for some bird watching. Then head on round the delightful headland to join a narrow path, which leads down to a glorious sandy strand. Stroll the sands, northwards, for 1 ½ miles / 2.5km until you come to a gap in the dunes, where a grassy track turns inland. (If the tide is high, walk the track, for a mile and a half, behind the narrow line of dunes, passing through two gates to reach the grassy track.) Follow the grassy track inland across the machair towards Ormiclate Castle.

Monkeyflower
& Meadowsweet

3 Walk on to where the track becomes a road. Turn right after the castle and follow the road south towards Bornish. Then turn right again onto a track immediately before the post box; it looks like a house access but the track swings right between a modern house and an old derelict one. Go through a gate and bear left, then pass through a second gate to meet a track coming down from Ormiclate Castle. Go straight on along a good grassy and sandy track through grazed machair. The track bends left, heading straight for St Mary's Church with Barra in the distance, then winds a bit with Loch Toronais to the left. Look for tufted duck, scaup and mergansers on the loch, with greylag geese grazing on the machair. Follow the track as it continues beside a fence to reach the track you walked at the outset of this ramble. Turn left to rejoin your car.

Practicals

Type of walk: Really delightful, level walk, with superb coastal views.

Distance: 6 ½ miles / 10.5km
Time: 4–5 hours
Maps: OS Explorer 453 / Landranger 22

NB: Part of this walk is on MOD land; it is a firing range, so obey any signs and flags which may be flying.

114

33

South Glendale (Gleann Dail bho Dheas) and Hartavagh (Thairteabhagh)

Park beside the road in South Glendale, grid ref. 791153. Take care not to block the road or obstruct passing places as the road is very narrow. Do not park in the bus turning area at the road end. To access this, leave the B888 at the left turn for Ludag, enjoying the scenic road and passing small quiet beaches. Immediately before the jetty, the road curves left, by-passing the start of the causeway to Eriskay, and ending at South Glendale.

This walk takes you over pathless low hills to **Hartavagh** (Thairteabhagh) where, in 1907, after the inhabitants were cleared from the west coast, several blackhouses were built. The children from the settlement used the track, and the bridge over the Abhainn Marulaig, on their way to and from school. This track but alas not the bridge is walked on your return.

Meall an Iasgaich from Cruachan, S. Glendale

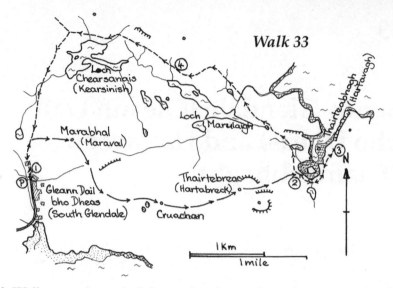

Walk 33

1 Walk up to the end of the road and pass through two gates by the last house. Follow the good track, uphill, until you near Loch na Brathad, away to the left. Leave the track and head, right, up the side of Maraval (Marabhal) (530 ft / 162m). There is no real path but the going is fairly easy. From the top, look out to the east to see Cruachan and Hartabreck (Thairtebreac), with the rocky coastline beyond. Here you might spot a golden eagle perhaps mobbed by peregrines. Descend Maraval on the south east side, heading for the broad col between Maraval and Cruachan, then climb up the ridge, keeping to the north of two small lochans, to Cruachan's summit. At the end of the ridge, descend east to cross the next col to begin your ascent up to the northern, and higher summit, of Hartabreck. Pause here to admire the superb views, particularly down to the narrow bay of Hartavagh. Bear right off the summit to make your way down the narrow valley leading to the head of Hartavagh where you meet the track from North Glendale (Gleann Dail bho Thuath).

Emperor Moth

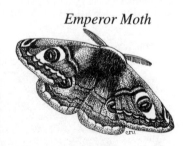

2 Turn right on the track and walk round the head of the bay, crossing the burn on a wooden plank bridge. Carry on round the bay, past

116

the tidal island, Eilean Dubh, before the track ends by several ruined blackhouses, with the jagged cliffs of Meall an Iasgaich beyond. The blackhouses were abandoned in 1927. Pause here where you might spot a basking shark feeding in the bay.

3 After a pause in this lovely corner of South Uist, return along the track round the head of Hartavagh and follow it uphill away from the west side of the bay. Look out for the little lochan covered with water lilies to your right. Soon, long Loch Marulaig

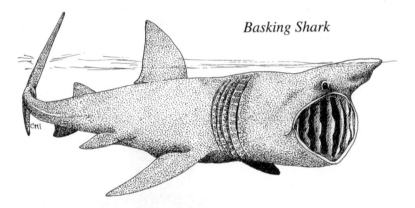

Basking Shark

comes into view on your left. Go on along the good track to come to the side of a burn, flowing out of the loch. The bridge, once used by the school children from Hartavagh has been down for many years and remains broken. In normal weather the burn can be crossed easily, just upstream of the track on a small stone-built dam, although this may be underwater and slippery if the burn is in spate. Then you may have to remove your boots and wade. Carry on along the track, which is clear and obvious, but can be very wet in places and has spread badly in the wettest areas. Pick the driest route across and continue as the track bends left round the higher ground towards the top of Loch Marulaig.

4 Carry on past the end of Loch Marulaig and then above Loch Kearsinish (Loch Chearsanais). As you pass the end of the latter, look left to see the path leading across the marshy area to South Glendale. The junction with the North Glendale path is not at all obvious, but the path leaves just before the peat workings and goes down to the left. If you reach the peat workings you can cut back across the hill to rejoin the path further down, as the going is fairly easy. The flat area by the loch foot is boggy and the path is a little unclear although it picks up again once you have crossed the burn. Follow the track back over the hill, from where you get lovely views down over South Glendale towards Eriskay and Barra. Return along the track to where you have parked.

*Peregrine dive-bombing
Golden Eagle*

Practicals

Type of walk: The two tracks are generally good and provide good walking, but take care where they are boggy and ill-maintained. There is no obvious path over the hills to Hartavagh.

Distance:	7 ½ miles / 12km
Time:	5 hours
Maps:	OS Explorer 453 / Landranger 31

34

Beinn Mhor and Hecla (Thacla), South Uist

Park beside the A865 near the turning to Howbeg (Tobha Beag) at grid reference 768348; the space is limited so park carefully.

South Uist's central mountainous area has two handsome large peaks, **Ben Mhor** (2034 ft / 620m) and **Hecla** (1990 ft / 606m) extending down to the rocky cliffs of the east coast.

A **raven** often soars and wheels at a great height, its wings motionless, its flight feathers extended like fingers. It seems to revel in air mastery. Its nest, a massive structure of sticks, heather stems and roots is built upon a ledge on some rocky outcrop or precipitous cliff-face and withstands most winter storms. When the birds were less persecuted, inland and lowland haunts were inhabited and the nest was usually built in some tall and ancient tree.

Beinn Corradail & Beinn Mhor from Hecla

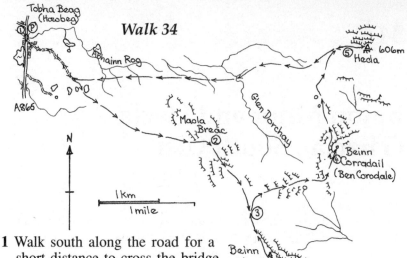

Walk 34

1 Walk south along the road for a short distance to cross the bridge over the River Roag (Abhainn Rog), then take a track leading off left beside houses. The track swings right and then left again and strikes off across the moor. Go through a gate and follow the track to its end, then carry on along a small footpath until it finally peters out in a bog. Strike off in a south-easterly direction towards Maola Breac ridge, passing between two lochans and keeping to higher ground where possible. Make your way up the slope to the ridge crest, joining a decent footpath that appears from the left. Listen for golden plovers calling as you climb, and look for the birds flying nearby.

2 Once on the ridge, bear right and carry on upwards. Pass a circle cairn on a subsidiary summit and follow the footpath along the ridge as it weaves from one side to the other round craggy bits. Rock doves fly around the crags as you approach. As you near the main cliffs, which edge the summit ridge, the path stays on the west side. Ahead is a clear view of the cairn on the south summit; at this point turn and look back to see the circle cairn surrounding the trig point on the main summit. Climb up to it and admire the splendid view. Then return to the subsidiary summit you crossed earlier. Keep a look out for wheatears and stonechats, which frequent the area.

3 Leave the main ridge here and head off down a side ridge to the right, aiming for the col, the Bealach Hellisdale (Sheiliosdail), between Beinn Mhor and Ben Corodale (Beinn Corradail). The going is fairly easy although take care because it is rocky in places.

120

The side of Ben Corodale ahead looks difficult and steep but is actually fairly straightforward. Head to the right from the col on a faint footpath and zig-zag your way up through the crags. It is remarkably easy going, at least when dry. Go over a small top to the Feith-bhealach and then on to the main summit, passing behind the cliffs.

4 From the summit cairn return to the Feith-bhealach and head down on the west side and round below the cliffs to the north-west ridge. Then go on down the north-west ridge to the bealach below Hecla, passing two small lochans, to climb the easy but steep side of Hecla's north-west ridge. Once on the ridge, swing right and follow the ridge to the summit, passing between rocksteps by easy breaks. The summit is spectacular, perched on a cliff outcrop. Wonderful views in all directions, including St. Kilda which looks huge and amazing. You may see ravens playing on the wind around the summit.

Starry

Saxifrage

5 Descend towards the bealach with lochans again, but before you reach it head off down the valley to the west. Stay towards the bottom of the steep slope on Maoladh Creag nam Fitheach and then head round its end. Cross Glen Dorchay (Gleann Dorchaidh), taking care when crossing the burn as it is a fairly deep channel. Pass through a line of old metal fence posts and continue round the end of Maola Breac to meet your outward track by the lochans. Retrace your steps along the path and track to rejoin the main road and your car.

Practicals

Type of Walk: Challenging. Suitable for experienced fell walkers who wear, and take, all the essential gear and are prepared to turn back if the weather deteriorates.

Distance: 11 ½ miles / 18km
Time: An all day excursion. Allow at least 7–8 hours
Maps: OS Explorer 453 / Landranger 22

35

East Gerinish (Caolas Liubharsaigh), South Uist

Park in a grassy lay-by close to the sea loch, Sheilavaig (Loch Sheileabhaigh), at the end of the road at East Gerinish, grid ref. 835402. To access this, leave the A865 at the signposted turn-off for Lochcarnan (Loch a' Charnain). This is the second left turn, if travelling south, after crossing the causeway from Benbecula to South Uist. At Lochcarnan take the right fork and continue for 3 ½ miles / 5.6km.

The **east coast of South Uist** is overlooked by mountains which rise to about 2000 ft. The coast is carved by sea lochs which provide sheltered anchorages for fishing boats and private craft. The west coast, in great contrast, is an area of high dunes and mile after mile of white sands.

Lily lochan, East Gerinish

1 Walk ahead along a wide grassy track, keeping to the left of a modern house and an old crofthouse. The track moves out into glorious heather moorland, with the Hecla range of hills ahead. Where the track comes beside an inland loch, ignore a left turn and continue past peat cuttings. On an island in the middle of the loch, honeysuckle flowers and willow and heather grow in profusion.

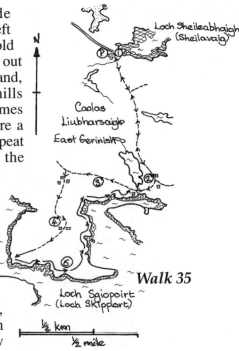

Walk 35

2 Follow the track as it passes beside a ruined crofthouse that overlooks an inlet of Loch Skipport (Loch Sgiopoirt), and then swings right past an area with sturdy walls, now crumbling in places. These walls surrounded the school, which is just a few stones but with steps and gates intact, when the area supported a largish population. One family who lived here sent 13 children to the school.

3 Stride on the raised track as it continues over wet moorland. Just before a rusty gate in a fence, carry on along the track as it swings uphill towards the ruin of another dwelling house that provides a grand view of Loch Skipport and the enclosing hills. Notice the lazy-beds running down to a bay on the loch. Strike across the moorland on an indistinct track (west) towards another crofthouse. Here a small stone barn has a roof thatched with heather.

4 Face the dwelling and leave by a causeway on the right. This skirts a craggy outcrop lush with heather, ferns and rhododendrons. Keep to the raised path as it swings right and then left, dropping downhill to a small bay opposite a jetty and a fish farm on the opposite bank of Loch Skipport. Walk left round the low headland, using good sheep tracks through the heather. When you come opposite a derelict pier with a splendidly-walled access track, move inland for a short distance.

123

5 Then continue with the lovely sea loch to your right, still making use of sheep tracks. Notice the many small inlets, most of which have an old boat still moored. Eventually you reach the ruins of the old school and here can pick up the grassy track to rejoin your car.

Honeysuckle &
Rosehips

Practicals

Type of walk: A pleasing walk taking you back a century in time. Good track for most of the way. No clear footpaths round the little headland but follow the edge of the loch.

Distance: 4 miles / 6.5km
Time: 3 hours
Maps: OS Explorer 453 / Landranger 22

36

Island of Eriskay (Eiriosgaigh), off South Uist

Park on the left, soon after you come onto Eriskay from the causeway, grid ref. 789119. To reach the island, leave the A865 at Daliburgh (Dalabrog), South Uist, and continue on the B888 until you can take the left turn for Ludag. Wind round the bay and then follow the road to cross the lovely Sound.

The Eriskay Love Lilt must be on most people's lips as they cross the causeway. At the beginning of the twentieth century the island became well known through the Gaelic song collection of Marjory Kennedy-Fraser, the best known of which is now the Love Lilt.

Work on the **causeway** began in May 2000 and the last ferry between Eriskay and Uist ran on July 12, 2001. It is 1650m long, and 720,000 tonnes of rock were used: 450,000 tonnes from a quarry above Glendale in South Uist and 270,000 tonnes from Eriskay where the access road

Acairseid Mhor, Eriskay

leading to the actual causeway was cut. The total cost of the project was £9.8 million. This included the ferry terminals for the circular ferry between Eriskay and Barra, the last link in the north/south communications in the Western Isles.

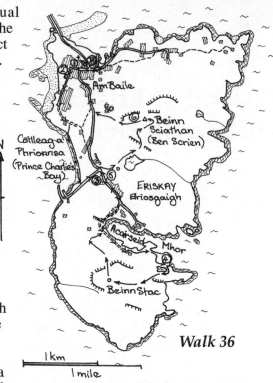

Walk 36

St Michael's Church, with its rounded north gable was founded in 1903. The church bell came from the German battleship, *Derflinger*, which was scuttled at Scapa Flow in Orkney. The altar is the bow of a lifeboat from the aircraft carrier *Hermes*, which came ashore after being washed overboard during an exercise off St Kilda. The ruins of the church which preceded the present one can be seen by the statue of the Lady of Fatima which is on the hillside as you walk up the main road on the way to the new ferry terminal for Barra.

On a line of crags above Acairseid there is a series of paintings on slates representing the **Stations of the Cross**. They were painted in 1970 on slates taken from the parish church of St Michael. A Stations of the Cross service is held annually at the paintings in Lent. The paintings are quite obvious from the top of Beinn Stac as each slate has a white cross painted above it. They start from the patch of trees at the head of Acairseid Mhor.

1 After a visit to St Michael's, wind right, to pass the school on the left. Ignore the first left turn (the main road) and carry on to wind down left to pass The Politician, opened in 1988. This is named

after a ship that sank off nearby Calvay Island (Calbhaig) in 1941. Among its cargo were 20,000 cases of whisky. Many of these were 'rescued' by the folk of Eriskay and the story has been told in Sir Compton Mackenzie's *Whisky Galore*.

2 Turn right after The Politician and walk on to pass the cemetery and the old cemetery and follow the lower road as it passes between two bungalows. Then go on down the track onto the beach (or follow a path above the beach). Stride the glorious stretch of shell-sand named Prince Charlie's Bay (Coilleag a' Phrionnsa). Here, in 1745, Bonnie Prince Charlie landed from France in his attempt to gather the clans for his rebellion. Three quarters of the way along the sands there is a stone cairn marking the spot. Carry on along the beach and through the dunes to reach the new road to the ferry terminal. Walk left and join the main road.

3 Turn right to follow the road leading round the head of Acairseid Mhor (the big harbour) and continue until you reach the end of the tarmac road. A footpath leads down to the left, across a bridge then a stile. Look for seals in the harbour as you walk along above the shore. Go through a gap in the fence and follow the fence round the shore. At the next fence turn inland and walk uphill beside it, crossing it at a stile. Walk down to Loch a' Chapuill before heading down to the tiny bay below where you may wish to sit and watch for otters.

4 Return to the lily-covered lochan and go on round it and under the cliffs at the far side. Bear left up the valley before turning right to head for the main summit of Ben Stack (Beinn Stac) (403 ft / 125m), where there is a cairn, and if you are lucky, sea eagles. Pause here for a superb view of Skye, Soay, Canna, Rum, Eigg and Muck. On a clear day you might also spot Tiree and Coll. From the summit head straight down towards the head of the bay (Acairseid Mhor). When you reach a fence, turn left to follow beside it and walk up to the corner where there is a gate. Go through and follow another fence that leads down to the road beside the harbour. Turn left to return to the road junction before the terminal.

5 Here climb right onto the grassy slopes and follow the way-marks over rocky outcrops and grassy hollows to pass to the left of a small reservoir. Continue on to pass to the left of Loch Crakavaig (Loch Cracabhaig). Then climb a grassy gully almost to the top of Ben Scrien (Beinn Sciathan) (609 ft / 185m). Just before the summit,

127

bear right to avoid a wet area and then climb the easy slope to the trig point on the top. Enjoy the wonderful view down to the causeway and the colourful houses of the island, scattered across a green apron. South Uist lies across the Sound, revealing its wide stretch of machair, which suddenly changes into heather moorland. In the distance stands Ben Mhor. Out to the east you might spot MacLeod's Tables on Skye.

6 Then head west, towards the Politician below, dropping down another grassy gully. At the fence walk right to go through a gate. Walk across the rough pastures towards the road. Don't forget to look for the Madonna on the hill.

Sea eagle

Practicals

Type of walk: This is a ramble to be savoured slowly. All of it is a pleasure to walk.

Distance: 6 miles / 9.8km
Time: 3–4 hours
Maps: OS Explorer 453 / Landranger 31

37

Eoligarry (Eolaigearraidh), Barra (Barraigh)

Park at Eoligarry Jetty, grid ref. 713077. To reach this drive past Barra airport and at the Y-junction take the right branch to the jetty where there is a small parking area, waiting room and toilets.

The view from the top of **Ben Scurrival** (Sgurabhal) (260 ft / 79m) is magnificent. Glorious sands seem to stretch for endless miles. A green sea merges into purple and cobalt blue. You can see Prince's Beach on Eriskay (walk 36), which seems just a short swim away, together with the island's Ben Scrien and Ben Stack. The houses of Ludag, the machair and hills, all on South Uist, lie to the north. Further away, the mountains of Skye and of the mainland of Scotland stand out clear in the crystal clear air. Close at hand Greian Head (Ceann Aird Ghrein) reveals its precipitous cliffs.

From the top of **Ben Eoligarry** (338 ft / 105m) you might spot a scheduled aircraft land and take off from the Traigh Mhor (or

Dun Scurrival, Eoligarry

Large Beach) below. If the tide is far out, look for tiny figures collecting cockles. From the little summit you have a good view of the narrow strip of dunes that separates the shell-sand bays of Traigh Eais and Traigh Mhor and you might ponder on how long it will take for the sea to overwhelm the narrow stretch of land or, on how long it will take to build up a wider strip. This low-lying isthmus between Eoligarry and the rest of Barra is composed of shingle and sand which has built up between what were originally two detatched islands to form a 'tombolo'.

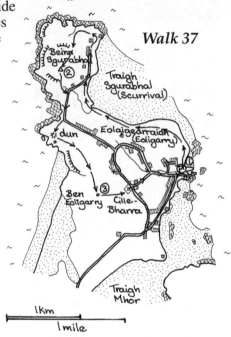

Cille-bharra, a twelth century church, has two chapels, of which one has been re-roofed. In the latter are medieval carved grave slabs and a replica of a ruinic stone; the original is in a museum in Edinburgh. It has been suggested that the stones from St Finbar's cell (sixth century) were used in the building of Cille-bharra. Sir Compton Mackenzie, the author of *Whisky Galore* is buried in this sunny, sheltered, peaceful corner of Barra.

1 From the parking area, walk north along the wonderful stretch of sand, Traigh Scurrival (Sgurabhal). As you pass a breeding colony of Arctic terns, ferocious protectors of their young, it is wise to carry your map on your head—for protection. Stroll on and look across the Sound of Barra to Fuday (Fuideigh) island, where sheep graze. Look for oyster-catchers, curlew, dunlin and turnstones running in and out of the seaweed. If the tide is too high or the wind makes it too difficult to walk the beach, follow the minor road, which runs parallel with the sands and ends at Scurrival Point. Pass through the gate at the end of the road and follow the track round to the right. Just before the next gate, at a cottage, follow signs to the left along the side of the fence to go through the gate at the end of the field. Bear slightly right to go through two more closely spaced gates. And then start your climb up the easy slopes of Ben Scurrival (260 ft / 79m) to reach the triangulation point.

2 Descend the south slope over outcrops of Gneiss to a gate onto the road and walk right (south). Pass through the next gate on the right and climb the slopes to see the Iron-age fort, Dun Scurrival (130 ft / 40m). Among the tumble of rocks on its wide flat top you can just discern a line of walling. In summer the mound is covered with thrift. Carry on along the continuing ridge and then ascend the easy slopes of Ben Eoligarry (338 ft / 102m) from where there is a spectacular view. As you ascend and descend this fine hill notice the enormous number of primroses that clothe the slopes.

3 Leave the summit, left (east) and descend to a gate at the far right of Cille-bharra. Pass through the gate and turn left. After a few metres, take the gate on the left to visit the cemetery. Enjoy this wonderful corner, and then walk down the lane opposite to return to the parking area.

Turnstones

Practicals

Type of walk: A very pleasing walk with some hill climbing but nothing too arduous. Wonderful views.

Distance: 4 ½ miles / 7.4km
Time: 3 hours
Maps: OS Explorer 452 / Landranger 31

131

38

Grianan and Beinn Verrisey (Bheireasaigh), Barra (Barraigh)

Park on a grassy lay-by, grid ref. 688033. To access this, leave Castlebay (Bagh a' Chasteil) and drive east and then north along the A888. Continue on the A-road as it winds west and park in the lay-by, on the left, just beyond Loch an Duin.

Loch an Duin has been dammed to provide water for the people who live in the northern part of the island. No dogs are allowed on this walk.

Aisled houses were constructed below ground. They were circular with a diameter of about 30 ft. They had an entrance passage about 24 ft. long. In the sunken area often ten or eleven stone spokes formed chambers. At the centre would have been a hearth. The house was probably roofed with turfs. Aisled houses were thought to be Pictish.

Grianan & Beinn Verrisey from Harteval

1 Walk down the road for a short distance to the track on the south side of Loch an Duin. Go through a ricketty gate and follow the lovely track beside the loch and up the valley beyond. The track leads round below Ben Obe (Beinn Ob), to your left, then swings right to the Obe River. Cross a stile over the fence and then the sturdy footbridge over the river. On the far bank, the track has dwindled to

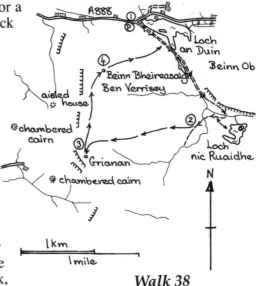

Walk 38

a footpath. Follow this to the right as it climbs gently up the hill. Near the top, leave the path to walk a little to your left for a view over Loch nic Ruaidhe and the remains of a dun on an island near the far end. Return to the path and continue as it leads down to another burn with a bridge. Cross and go on up the valley to your left.

2 As the path reaches the crest of a small hill, look to your right where a little narrow path leaves it to head off uphill. Take this path and stay with it as it winds up towards the ridge of hills, which make a backbone for the island. Nearly halfway up, the path disappears into a boggy area. Make for a cairn on the nearby small hilltop then continue straight up hill. At the ridge, turn left to walk along to the main summit of Grianan. The view is spectacular,

Common Hawker Dragonfly

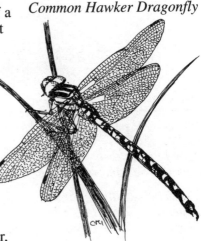

133

down the valley to Borve (Borgh), with Heaval (Sheabhal) and Harteval (Thartabhal) to your left. Look especially for the chambered cairn on the col before Beinn Mhartainn and the ruined chambered cairn down the valley above the Duarry Burn.

3 Turn north and follow the ridge down over the col to an intermediate summit. Take time to look down on the ruined aisled house just below, near the head of the burn. Continue along the ridge, keeping to the right to avoid steep ground. Cross the next col, stepping over a broken fence, and climb up to the summit of Beinn Verrisey (650 ft / 197m), marked by a tiny cairn. Pause to enjoy the lovely views north over Loch an Duin to South Uist. Look for golden plovers on the grassy slopes.

4 Head downhill to the north east, aiming for Loch an Duin. The way becomes quite steep on the lower slopes so care is needed. Once you reach the track, turn left to retrace your outward route beside the loch. In summer this area is alive with dragon and damselflies. Look particularly for common darter and common hawker dragonflies. Return through the gate to where you have parked.

Kestrel

Practicals

Type of walk: Easy walking along the track. A little more adventurous and rough over Beinn Verrisey.

Distance: 3 miles / 5km
Time: 2 hours
Maps: OS Explorer 452 / Landranger 31

39

Heaval (Sheabhal) and Harteval (Thartabhal), Barra

Park in the car park about 1 mile above Castlebay, grid ref. 678987. The parking area is just below the top of the hill on the right as you drive east on the A888.

Barra's capital is **Castlebay** (Bagh a' Chaisteil). Around the shores of its beautiful, natural harbour straggle attractive houses, shops, a hospital, a church and the community school with its library, swimming pool and other leisure facilities. In the late nineteenth century huts and bothies were scattered around the shores of the bay and in these huge catches of herring were gutted, salted and packed for distribution throughout Europe. Overlooking the town stands Heaval, Barra's highest peak, 1,260 ft / 383m.

Dominating the bay is the dramatic **Kisimul Castle** (Caisteal Chiosmuil) built in the fifteenth century by the MacNeils. Over the centuries more MacNeil chieftains became overlords of the island. In 1840 General Roderick MacNeil sold the island and its castle to settle his debts. In 1937 Robert Lister MacNeil, a member of a Canadian branch of the MacNeil clan bought the castle, and

Kisimul Castle, Barra

Walk 39

much of the island. He restored the castle, between 1956–70. Today it is leased to Historic Scotland for a thousand years for an annual rent of £1 and a bottle of whisky. It is regularly opened to the public. In 2003 Ian MacNeil decided to give up 9,000 acres (much of the island of Barra). He gifted it to the Scottish Executive, with the intention of its eventually being handed over to the community, free of charge.

In 1954 the Welcome Home fund for Seamen erected the marble statue of the **Madonna and Child** on the slopes of Heaval.

1 From the car park, cross the A-road, turn right and walk a short distance along the road until you reach a small footbridge over the ditch and a stile over the fence. Cross these and bear left round the side of Heaval. There are several small footpaths although none continue for long; in spite of this the walking is fairly easy. Continue on round the hillside to climb a lovely grassy ramp between the lines of crags. This brings you round to the north-west ridge overlooking Borve (Borgh)

2 Turn right to climb up the much more gently sloping ridge to gain the summit. Continue along the summit ridge to the trig point at the far end and pause to admire the views down to Castlebay

Cuckoo

with Kisimul Castle, as well as across to Vatersay (Bhatarsaigh) and the islands to the south.

3 To continue, return along the summit ridge but instead of descending as you came up, bear to the right towards Harteval and an intermediate, unnamed summit. Make your way down to the col and pass between the small peaty pools before climbing the short distance to the cairn on the intermediate summit. From here the route onto Harteval is clear. Pass straight on down to the next col, which lies a little lower than the previous one, then follow the path up the steep end of Harteval. Pause by the summit cairn to appreciate the views.

4 Descend by the same route to the col immediately below Harteval. From here, instead of retracing your footsteps over the intermediate summit and back to Heaval, bear off round the hillside to your left and follow the many sheep tracks. This will bring you round below the intermediate summit and the col below Heaval. Try not to lose too much height. After some way you should pick up clearer footpaths which gradually converge before bringing you round a last section to overlook the main footpath up Heaval.

5 From here you will be very close to the white marble statue of the Madonna and Child. From the statue, follow the main footpath, which leads straight down the hill, zig-zagging over the steeper areas. As you near the base of the hill, leave the footpath to bear right over the heathery turf to reach the stile and footbridge that you crossed on the outward route. Cross these and turn right to return to your car.

Practicals

Type of walk: An exhilarating and challenging climb, suitable for those who like being in the hills and finding their way over indistinct paths.

Distance: 3 miles / 5km
Time: 2 hours
Maps: OS Explorer 452 / Landranger 31

40

Vatersay (Bhatarsaigh) Off Barra

Park in the small car park just beyond the old school and on the other side of the road, grid ref. 635954. To reach Vatersay leave Castlebay on Barra and head west on the A888. After three-quarters of a mile take a left turn, signposted Nask (Nasg) and Vatersay, to drive on to the causeway linking the two islands. Continue southwards, following the shore of Bagh Chornaig, then round Vatersay Bay (Bagh Bhatarsaigh) until you pass the old school and reach the parking area just beyond, on the left.

The causeway was built in 1990 at a cost of three million pounds. Previously, **cattle from Vatersay** had to swim the often treacherous Sound of Vatersay to reach Barra. Though access to the island is now so easy the lovely little island remains quiet and peaceful. In spring it is a riot of primroses and a place where you might hear and even see corncrakes. The machair supports red and white clover,

Sandray from South Beach, Vatersay

kidney vetch, pansies, and field gentians. Watch out for buzzards and the much larger golden eagle, the presence of both often given away by being mobbed by smaller birds.

'On 28th September 1853 the ship *Annie Jane* with emigrants from Liverpool to Quebec was totally wrecked in this bay and three-fourths of the crew and passengers numbering about 350 men, women and children drowned and their bodies interred here.' So says the fading inscription on the tall granite monument that stands in the dunes beside West Beach (Traigh Siar). And below is added 'And the sea gave up her dead that were in it'. The memorial marks the burial site of those who died in a tragic shipwreck during a terrible storm. The victims were emigrants from Britain, volunteers, skilled craftsmen and their families on the their way to begin a new life building the railway system in Canada.

The Vatersay dun is one of a string of duns found along the west coast of the Western Isles. They were probably built around the last century BC and the first and second centuries AD as fortified dwelling places.

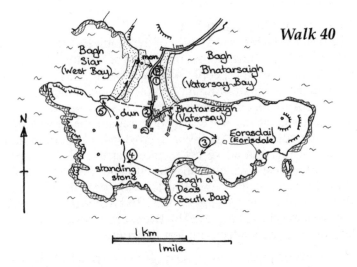

Walk 40

1 Walk on along the narrow road that runs the length of the 'waist' of the island, with dunes on either side. These border extensive strands of silver sand. Make for the township of Vatersay, where the council has built wooden houses for fishermen and their families and where there are several new houses. A large herd of well fed cattle wander the slopes about the houses and over the machair.

2 Once in the village, bear left as the road divides and head for East Beach. Take the track off to the right by the edge of the houses, leading towards an isolated house. Before reaching this house, take the track leading left to follow round the side of Ben Cuier (Beinn Chuidhir) towards a saddle of higher ground. From the saddle, bear round to the south, keeping to the west of the Eorisdale (Eorasdail) Burn and passing, away to your left, the ruins of the settlement of Eorisdale. This was one of the four original villages, established after the Land Raids of 1909. These raids were carried out by landless folk who were unable to eke out a living. It was inhabited as late as the 1970s.

Dune Pansies

3 Make your way through the dunes to the beautiful white sand beach of the South Bay (Bagh a' Deas). Enjoy the superb views across the Sound of Sandray (Sanndraigh), once occupied by the people who had been unable to eke out a living on the island of Mingulay—you can just spot a small part of the latter. Walk on along the beach and make your way, with care, over the rocks at the western end to regain the grassy machair. Where the coast is broken by a steep-sided inlet, climb up along the side of this and strike off to the west to follow the periodic way-marker posts, which lead you into and then along a shallow valley. To your left, just behind the low ridge, can be seen a standing stone silhouetted against the skyline. Today it is used as a gatepost but once it may have been used by Bronze Age peoples as a meeting place or even associated with fertility rites.

4 Turn right here to pass round the ridge below Ben Rulibreck (Beinn Ruilibreac). Two stiles lead you over the closely spaced fences and on to the footpath to the summit of Dun Vatersay (165 ft / 50m). Once it would have had massive double drystone walls, with

140

steps between, leading up to galleries. Little remains of the dun today, as, over the centuries, the stone has been used for other purposes. Admire the views from here across the sandy expanse of West Beach to the northern part of island, and the excellent defensible position of the dun.

5 Descend the dun on the south side and pass round to your right below the crags to cross a stile over the fence before following the footpath down to the sea. Bear right and make your way down onto the sand of West Beach at the first opportunity. Walk north, almost to the end of the bay, and then pass, right, through a natural break in the dunes and a footpath leading to the plain monument. It is a moving tribute to the *Annie Jane*. Continue on a good footpath across the machair to a gate in the fence opposite the car park.

Velvet & Common Scoters

Practicals

Type of walk: A walk not to be missed. Generally easy walking, with a steady climb to the dun.

Distance: 4 miles / 6km
Time: 2–3 hours
Maps: OS Explorer 452 / Landranger 31

Clan Walks

A series of walks described by Mary Welsh, covering some of the most popular holiday areas in the Scottish Highlands and Islands.

Titles published so far include:

1. 44 WALKS ON THE ISLE OF ARRAN
2. WALKING THE ISLE OF SKYE
3. WALKING WESTER ROSS
4. WALKS IN PERTHSHIRE
5. WALKING THE WESTERN ISLES
6. WALKING ORKNEY
7. WALKING SHETLAND
8. WALKING THE ISLES OF ISLAY, JURA AND COLONSAY
9. WALKS ON CANNA, RUM, EIGG AND MUCK
10. WALKS ON TIREE, COLL, COLONSAY AND A TASTE OF MULL
11. WALKING DUMFRIES AND GALLOWAY
12. WALKING ARGYLL AND BUTE
13. WALKING DEESIDE, DONSIDE AND ANGUS
14. WALKING THE TROSSACHS, LOCH LOMONDSIDE AND THE CAMPSIE FELLS
15. WALKING GLENCOE, LOCHABER AND THE GREAT GLEN

OTHER TITLES IN PREPARATION

Books in this series can be ordered through booksellers anywhere. In the event of difficulty write to Clan Books, The Cross, DOUNE, FK16 6BE, Scotland.